TAROT OF CEREMO

LON MILO DUQUETTE

TAROT
of
CEREMONIAL
MAGICK

A PICTORIAL SYNTHESIS OF
THREE GREAT PILLARS OF MAGICK:
ENOCHIAN, GOETIA, ASTROLOGY

A companion text to the deck
published by U. S. Games Systems

SAMUEL WEISER, INC.

York Beach, Maine

This edition first published in 1995 by
Samuel Weiser, Inc.
Box 612
York Beach Maine 03910-0612

Library of Congress Cataloging-in-Publication Data
DuQuette, Lon Milo.
    Tarot of ceremonial magick : a pictorial synthesis of three great pillars of magick : astrology, enochian magick, Goetia / by Lon Milo DuQuette.
        p.   cm.
    Includes bibliographical references and index.
    1. Tarot.   2. Enochian magic.   3. Cabala.   4. Divination.
I. Title.
BF1879.T2D87   95-14649
133.3'2424—dc20   CIP
ISBN 0-87728-764-3
CCP

Typeset in 10 point Plantin.
Printed in the United States of America.

03 02 01 00 99 98 97 96 95
10 9 8 7 6 5 4 3 2 1

The paper used in this publication meets the minimum requirements of the American National Standard for Permanence of Paper for Printed Library Materials Z39.48–1984.

Contents

Figures

Foreword

You are presumably reading this book because you have an interest in Tarot, or in one or more of its cognate areas. You could be an Astrologer, or a student of Magic(k) or the Qabalah. It may be that you are familiar with some of Lon's previous works—*The Way of the Secret Lover*[1] (in which an early version of the major arcana of the *Tarot of Ceremonial Magick* appeared), or the more recent *Magick of Thelema*.[2] You might be a Witch wishing to expand your comparative-magick skills, or a Thelemite desiring some much-needed help in understanding Aleister Crowley. You *may* even—lucky you!—know Lon, and wish to draw from his fountain of wit, erudition, and above all, magical sanity. The book you are reading is Lon's commentary to his tarot deck, the *Tarot of Ceremonial Magick*. He describes this deck as "a pictorial synthesis of three great pillars of Magick: Astrology, Enochian, Goetia," and you will find this ambitious promise fulfilled in both the deck, and in this companion volume. I am convinced that whatever your interests in the Arts Arcane, you will find your horizons broadened, your knowledge deepened, and your understanding heightened by the material in this deck and book, and by the Magus-friendly manner in which it is presented to you.

---

1. One of four books Lon co-authored with Christopher Hyatt (Scottsdale, AZ: New Falcon Publications, 1991).
2. *The Magick of Thelema* (York Beach, ME: Samuel Weiser, 1993).

The tarot is many things. Among them: It explains both the origin and *telos* of our present Universe, and of past and future Universes as well. It schematizes the essential and necessary relationships that make up Manifestation. It is a system of self- (and Self-) knowledge. It provides a glimpse into the Mind of Creation. It is a sound oracle. Finally, it is an effective and affordable psychotherapist. As you either already know or will soon understand, the tarot is intimately related to the twenty-two letters of the ancient Hebrew alphabet, and to their evolution, as described in that venerable Semitic filing system known as the Qabalah and its iconographic abbreviation, the Tree of Life.

This book is the distillation of decades of study, research, meditation and ritual enactment by the author. I believe it represents one of the most exciting breakthroughs in the tarot, in its arrangement and presentation of several occult systems relating to that elegant, versatile and indispensable Map of Consciousness, the Qabalah.

For many Western occultists (myself once among them), the approach to tarot developed by Aleister Crowley and presented in the *Thoth Tarot Deck* and its companion volume *The Book of Thoth*[3] are the last words on that subject. We find in Crowley's written and visual materials a grand synthesis, explaining Astrology, Alchemy, Numerology, Qabalah, color symbolism, and Geomancies Eastern and Western. *The Book of Thoth* both delineates the relationships among these branches of the One Tree of Metaphysical Knowledge, and for our right brain's benefit, illustrates them through the evocative aesthetic of Frieda Harris' faithful executions of Crowley's designs for the cards. Many of us came to Crowley's system after years of working with other decks and approaches. Most of us still using the Crowley Tarot as our deck of choice would, I believe, deny that any improvement on Crowley's material was conceivable or necessary, let alone possible.

---

3. *The Book of Thoth* (York Beach, ME: Samuel Weiser, 1991, and the *Thoth Tarot Deck* (Samuel Weiser/Urania Verlag, 1986).

However, there are some features of our allegiance to *The Book of Thoth* which we usually leave unspoken:

The bootless hours spent poring over our ragged, earmarked, coffeestained and, eventually, looseleafed copies of the book, and our unsuccessful attempts to wrest some applicable information out of statements like the following example, on the 9 of Cups:

> Jupiter in Pisces is indeed good fortune, but only in the sense of complete satiety. The fullest satisfaction is merely the matrix of a further putrefaction; there is no such thing as absolute rest.[4]

or, on the Ace of Disks:

> This card is thus an affirmation of the identity of Sol and Terra—and that will be best understood by those who have punctually practiced "Liber Resh" for the necessary number of years, preferably in such Hermitages as those of the Sahara Desert, where the Sun and the Earth can soon be instinctively recognized as living Beings, one's constant companions in a Universe of pure Joy.[5]

There is also our mystification at some of Crowley's more inspired (or outrageous) leaps of logic, and our last-ditch employment of tertiary interpretive devices including, but not limited to, several multi-lingual dictionaries, two ouija boards, and a pendulum. The sublime beauty of *The Book of Thoth*—its use of so many diverse magical systems—is also the inherent limitation in its usefulness for many of us. We lose track of the point, seduced by Crowley's masterful presentation of virtually every critical magical, mythological and spiritual tradition of East and West.

A related drawback is that most of us serious working occultists are perforce specialists. Unlike Crowley, who was very possibly the last magical genius and Renaissance man of this century, we

---

4. *The Book of Thoth*, p. 186.
5. *The Book of Thoth*, pp. 211–212.

tend to limit ourselves to one or a very few magical subsystems, such as Astrology, or Ceremonial Magick, or the practice of Goetia or the Enochian system. Even in the (sadly few) intellectually-inclined pockets of modern Witchcraft we find the study and use of the Qabalah as the foundation and keystone, the magical language by which we translate, and thereby begin to understand, the traditional teachings of Wicca. We choose to restrict our magical practices to avoid the dreaded dilletantism which would render us spiritually impotent, spinning uselessly on our Astrals. Because of this self-imposed limitation, it is for many of us an insurmountable challenge to derive the specific datum that would be most valuable to us from our readings in *The Book of Thoth*, a sometimes over-whelming compilation of material that underscores Crowley's unique status among occultists as well as our own modern meta-physical limitations. Each of these difficulties is addressed, and to a great extent resolved, by the *Tarot of Ceremonial Magick*.

Lon is a Thelemite, but the *Tarot of Ceremonial Magick* is far from being a reworking of Aleister Crowley's material. Nor is it Lon's intent to fling Crowley off the tarot pedestal upon which so many of us have placed him. Lon's deck may be used exclusively as a complete and exciting Tarot system in its own right; but you may also wish to avail yourself of the opportunities inherent in the potent conjunction of *The Book of Thoth* and the *Tarot of Ceremo-nial Magick*—since both derive from the Qabalah, how could you not?—but what you will find in the latter is an utterly simple and therefore astounding rearrangement of the diverse traditions pre-sented in the former, in a way which renders them immediately accessible to the student. At a glance, you will see the Zodiacal, Enochian, Ceremonial, Goetic, Tattvic and Elemental components of each specific card, as well as the unique spot that card occupies in each of those systems, and its particular relationship to the other cards. And *this* in the space of a few moments!

Allow me to share this embarrassing story by way of illus-tration: I have been an astrologer (and an occasional profes-sional teacher and counselor) as well as a student of tarot for over two decades. Although I had used *The Book of Thoth* almost exclusively for 15 years, I had never seen[6] how the number cards of the minor arcana are to be arranged to form the complete wheel of the zodiac. Lon pulled out the 2–3–4 of Wands [the first, second and third decans of Aries], the 5–6–7 of Disks [the decans of Taurus], the 8–9–10 of Swords [the decans of Gemini] and the 2–3–4 of Cups [the decans of Cancer]—and so on! I was dumbfounded. And yet there these zodiacal relationships were revealed in the composition of his cards for any to see—and this in the hurly-burly of the U.S. book industry's largest trade show, *not* an atmosphere conducive to subtle thought. If this one minor example indicates the degree of personal breakthrough I experienced, under those circumstances, imagine the leaps in consciousness which will become available to you in your orderly study as you explore Lon's material.

Among the many aspects of this deck I sincerely appreciate is its lack of pretension. Lon has an ability to transmit profound truths with style and quiet humor—elements usually lacking in contemporary occult writers. Just look at the Small Cards, where he has the 2 of Cups, the Lord of Love, as two ice-cream sundaes. The 7 of Cups, the Lord of Illusory Success ("Debauch" in Crowley), is shown as a stack of martinis. In the 4 of Wands—the Lord of Perfected Works—the wands form the masonic square and compasses, surmounted by the All-Seeing Eye (of Horus). The wands of the 6 stretch out to the horizon and allude to the

---

6. Or, more accurately, "had not remembered." It was recently pointed out to me that not only does Crowley, in "A Description of the Cards of the Tarot," *The Equinox* I(7–8) (1912, reprinted York Beach, ME: Samuel Weiser, 1992; also reprinted as *Tarot Divination* (Samuel Weiser, my copy 1985), explicitly spell out the decanate-small card sequence, but that one may even, working at it a bit, figure it out from "the Divisions of the Zodiac" map in Cheiro's *Book of Numbers* (New York: Arco, 1980). I should therefore delete this entire paragraph from these introductory comments since there was no purpose to be served in gratuitous self-humiliation. Quite the contrary! Having read *both* of these works in years past, and having had that particular bit of information drop out of my consciousness, I believe the example serves to emphasize Lon's efficient and accessible arrangement of the material (astrological, in this case).

planetary ruler, Jupiter's function as the lord of expansion. In the
10 of that suit, the Lord of Oppression, the wands form the bleak
gate of a medieval dungeon. And the major arcana! Not only do
the personae depicted form the basis of an entirely self-referential
system in itself (and one elaborate occult joke I'm hoping Lon will
fully reveal to his readers), but the other keys exhibit Lon's own
unique teaching method. Just wait until you get a look at XIII. I
guarantee this to be the only Death card to elicit giggles; it also
illustrates some overlooked aspects of this most grim of Atus.

★   ★   ★

I'd like to turn a bit to what philosophers and theologians call the
Problem of Evil.[7] I'm not a ceremonial magician of either the High
or Goetic sort. I've never been particularly successful in the sum-
moning of angelic or demonic beings—unless, of course, you count
those whose sensibilities are acutely responsive to the sound of cat
food cans being opened. However, as students of the Qabalah—the
Tree whose roots pierce the depths of existence, and whose
branches brush the very heavens—we encounter the range of Manifestation, at least academically. In a comprehensive spiritual system
such as the Qabalah, one which touches (in Douglas Adams'
words) Life, the Universe, and Everything, there is nothing left
unexplored. The birth-cries of galaxies and the unobserved dance
of subatomic particles alike are grist for our rabbinical mills.
Abstract human principles such as Truth and Justice—our species'
highest Ideals—are there represented. In the Wicca, there is nothing
in our experience of Being which is "unworthy" of or excluded
from our scrutiny: "The aware Wicca does not reject the world
from fear of it. She holds it firmly in her grasp and wrests from it

7. I wish to acknowledge, with love and gratitude, my dear friend Richard
Patz for our ongoing discussion of several years' duration on this and many
related subjects, and for the insights he always provides me.

its secrets."[8] This is in fact our job—to observe and to study, in hopes that we will be vouchsafed a true understanding of the natures and relationships comprising every aspect of Manifestation. This is, of course, the occupation of several lifetimes; but your serious occultist is in for the long haul. It falls to us to seek out and embrace every facet of life as it comes; everything to us is sacred, and each particular occasion of Being participates in, and has as its origin and end, the Divine. I struggle when this philosophical and spiritual certainty collides with the repellent: how could we have allowed the Holocaust to happen, or the earlier atrocities of the Holy Office of the Inquisition? Why are there babies born with AIDS? Why do Tibetan Lamas die of cancer? Why do we suffer? Why are there ticks? Why was I—one of the most scrupulously honest people I know—robbed yesterday? Vague invocations of karmic fulfillment beg serious questions; see Ken Wilbur's magnificent *True Grace and Grit*. The Buddha's answer is cold comfort indeed to those of us consigned to being-in-the-world to learn the lessons of Assiah. Although I cannot presume to cut this particular millenia-old Gordian knot in the space of a few brief paragraphs, step back a pace with me to view, as a student of the Qabalah, the larger canvas of Creation.

The present world in which we live was not the first; learned rabbis, scriptural commentators, have informed us throughout the centuries that The Creator(s) tried Its (Their) Hand(s) at a number of attempts at Manifestation. The creative force emanated from the source, spilling "down" and "out" to fill and overflow each of the ten succeeding "vessels" of form (the ten Sephiroth of the Tree of Life) to arrive, finally, as our lovely world. In the first attempts the vessels weren't "strong" enough to hold it. Those vessels shattered, and their shards—the Shells, Harlots, or Qliphoth—became the substance of what we commonly term "demons." This is one view—and I beg the reader's forgiveness for this simplistic presentation. These Shells have served, for

---

8. From the soon-to-be-republished *Wicca: The Ancient Way* (Lilburn, GA: IllumiNet Press, 1994).

countless æons, as the flies in an otherwise harmoniously-appointed ointment. Throughout the centuries, their names, appearances, job descriptions and places within the creative hierarchy have been analyzed by Qabalists. These energies are as much a part of the correspondences aligned with each Sephira as all the other spiritual entities related to the Tree of Life—the archangels, angels, planetary intelligences, mythological personages, divine entities and others, each belonging to its proper station.

I introduce this topic because the *Tarot of Ceremonial Magick* forces us to confront it. And although I have never subscribed to the rose-colored glasses approach to metaphysics—what my own spiritual teacher calls the "Hello Sky, Hello Clouds, Hello Fuzzy Bunny" school of occultism—the presence of the sigils belonging to the evil genii on the trump cards was disturbing to me. It was, in fact, the only aspect of the deck to which I could not initially commit my unequivocal enthusiasm. I engaged Lon in immediate discussion of this subject, there at the book fair where he first showed me the deck, and continuing in our sporadic but ongoing correspondence. In a letter to me written in mid-fall of 1993, Lon discusses the sigils of the two classes of genii appearing on each major arcana card. One class, he wrote, is representative of the House of Mercury, an important class of symbols inexplicably overlooked by virtually every writer except Crowley in his "Liber 231."[9] Of the other class of sigil, Lon wrote:

> ... The abode of the second genii of each trump is not a house but a prison. These sigils often appear as distorted, unbalanced or corrupted versions of those found in the Houses of Mercury. No matter how unsightly or unpleasant these fellows may be, they are a magical fact of life. We don't have to like them, and we certainly don't have to exalt them, but they are a part of the great tapestry and our understanding of the universe and ourselves will remain incomplete if we ignore

---

9. See Appendix Five.

them. Worse, by ignoring them they have the nasty
habit of getting out and working mischief.

It is my opinion that the placement of the correct
sigils of the geniis of the Domarum Mercurii and the
placement of the sigils of the geniis of the Carcerorum
Qliphoth upon the same tarot trump is an appropriate
way to magically display the entire spectrum of meaning inherent in the card. Furthermore, to a certain
extent, I believe that the same forces reside in the
trumps of every tarot deck whether they are overtly
symbolized or not. At least in my deck a balance is
struck and the great symbol of the Atu stands ever on
guard over the prisoner in the next box.

I find myself in agreement with Lon. These beings have never simply gone away upon a lack of acknowledgment. Furthermore, Lon's
deck has offered me the beginnings of a profound insight into
understanding the problem of evil in the world—the same insight
one may infer from the white-and-black checkered floor of the
Temple of Malkuth, or of the masonic lodge. If the progress of the
major arcana depicts, on one level, the spiritual evolution of the
human soul throughout its lifetime(s), then the undeniable encoun-
ters with what is commonly termed "evil"[10] become yet another
tool by which we may shape our lives, to an end *dulce et utile*, "as
a carpenter shapes wood." While the suffering of "evil" in life is
unavoidable, we can come to understand that our responses to that
evil are not; on each occasion, we are graced with the opportunity
to grow in awareness through self-knowledge. Truly won self-
knowledge affords us the discipline to regulate our responses and
to preserve our integrity in the face of evil. Most importantly, it is
through awareness alone that spiritual evolution—the magician's
ultimate and only aim—is maintained or even possible. Finally, as
all good Hermeticists know, "as above, so below" (and as within,

---

10. "Evil" is in quotation marks because a seeming "evil" is often anything
but, and *vice versa*; please refer to the formula of Copper, "external splendour and internal corruption" (Crowley, *The Book of Thoth*, p. 199).

so without): if we can find the honesty, courage and love, and trust in the divine plan enough to seek out and acknowledge our individual shadows, then there is no reason why we must be forced to face them outside ourselves, in the world of Form. Any predictive astrologer will tell you this. Awareness is the key, and it is that most valuable key which Lon has here provided occultists in our ongoing confrontation with the problem of evil. We owe him a great debt; thank you, Lon.

—Judith Hawkins
March 1995 CE

Preface

In 1856, Alphonse Louis Constant (Éliphas Lévi) published what was to become one of the most influential works on ceremonial magic ever written, *Rituel de la haute magie.*[1] In Chapter 22, "The Book of Hermes," he publicly revealed for the first time that...

> "...the twenty-two keys of the Tarot are the twenty-two letters of the primitive kabalistic alphabet..." [2]

Students of Western Hermeticism and Christian mysticism had long suspected a qabalistic foundation to the Tarot of the Bohemians, but such things were seldom spoken of publicly. The uninitiated were left to speculate about mysterious societies of qabalistic magicians who were bound by terrible oaths never to reveal their secret knowledge to the profane. Indeed such colorful suppositions may not have been too far-fetched. Strict secrecy had long been the tradition among Hebrew qabalists, and one need only recall the horrors of a millennium of religious intolerance to realize that indiscretion in spiritual matters is often bad for one's health.

Lévi's *Rituel* appeared to boldly settle the question of the tarot keys once and for all. However, a close examination of his sequence of the keys *vis-à-vis* the Hebrew alphabet disclosed curious inconsistences, and for students already familiar with fundamental qabalistic texts such as the *Sepher Yetzirah*, serious

---

1. Part II of *Dogme et ritual de la haute magie* (1854–56), translated by A.E. Waite as *Transcendental Magic* (York Beach, ME: Samuel Weiser, 1993).
2. *Transcendental Magic*, p. 386.

questions were raised. It appeared as if Lévi wrote a perfectly logical (and qabalistically correct) treatise, then simply threw the descriptive paragraphs slightly out of sequence. Such obvious devices led his contemporary readers to conclude that Lévi himself was a formal initiate and this was his way of revealing secrets without technically breaking his oaths.

The late 1800s saw a proliferation of interest in all things occult. Magical and metaphysical societies sprang up throughout Europe and England, and obscure texts which had gathered dust for centuries were translated and published. Foremost among these were *The Book of the Sacred Magic of Abra-Melin the Mage*, the five books of the *Lemegeton*, and an entire body of work by the great 16th century English magus, Dr. John Dee.

By 1900 the most influential magical society of the day, the Golden Dawn, had begun to disintegrate, and the publication of the order's essential teachings in 1909 signaled the end of an age in which secret societies monopolized the inner spiritual teachings of the West. Nevertheless, today the secrets are still securely guarded; not by societies and oaths, but by the subtle profundity of the teachings themselves, and the unwillingness of all but the most tenacious students to devote even a little time and attention to the quest. It is indeed ironic that in an era when bookstore shelves overflow with the secret teachings of the ages, the secrets are more deeply hidden than ever.

— Lon Milo DuQuette
Newport Beach, California

Acknowledgments

The author would like to first express his heartfelt thanks to James Wasserman and Christopher S. Hyatt, Ph.D., whose support and encouragement in the early years of the project helped to manifest the *Tarot of Ceremonial Magick*.

Special thanks also go to Constance Jean DuQuette for her artistic assistance and interpretive insight; Stuart Kaplan of U.S. Games Systems, Inc.; Judith Hawkins; Hymenaeus Beta, Frater Superior of Ordo Templi Orientis; Poke Runyon; Rick D. Potter; Steve and Judy Abbott; Scott and Caryle Fineburg; and Doug and Karen James.

Introduction

Why Another Tarot Deck?

Next to the signs of the zodiac, the tarot cards are the most popular and recognizable symbols of the occult arts. The last twenty years have witnessed such a proliferation of new decks that many occult and "New Age" bookstores have literally had to knock out walls to provide display space to accommodate the ever-expanding inventory of new decks and related books. Even mainstream book outlets have surprisingly large tarot sections. One can even receive a tarot reading anytime, day or night, from a wide variety of twenty-four hour telephone tarot readers who tout their services in slickly produced television commercials.

With such an explosion of interest in tarot one would think that scholarship on the subject would be at an all-time high. Curiously enough, for the most part this is not the case. With very few exceptions the new decks are simply novelty versions of the classic designs or else not tarot cards at all, but collections of images significant to a wide spectrum of disciplines, philosophies, or cultures. Such projects are a wonderful form of artistic expression and I hope that the popularity of medium never wanes. Nevertheless, these products reveal little or nothing of the profound mysteries concealed just below the surface in each of the 78 cards of the tarot—mysteries of the creation of the universe; mysteries of the human soul. An analogy would be if the Rosetta Stone were famous only for its color and hardness.

Fortune-telling can be fun, and I will not argue the fact that the tarot's great popularity stems largely from its use as a parlor game. I confess that I have on more than one occasion attempted to liven

up a gathering by cracking out the tarot cards and telling the cred-
ulous souls what they want to hear. Oddly enough I seldom know
at the time that it *is* what they want to hear. Even in this cavalier
application, the cards seem to focus natural psychic abilities. I
have great respect for the abilities of a talented reader of tarot.

But the cards are much more than 78 "buzz words" which can
be shuffled and randomly chosen to answer specific questions.
The tarot is a living mandala; a graphic, pictorial breakdown of
the mechanics of creation.[1] If the unfortunate implications of theology could be ignored, we could call the tarot the picture-book of
the mind of God. There are other such divine picture-books. The
64 hexagrams of the *I Ching* form an exquisite system that paral-
lels the tarot in many respects. It is based upon the sublime principles of the *Tao Te Ching* and is particularly suited to the subtleties
of Eastern thought.

The Hebrew Qabalah[2] forms the foundation upon which the
Western Hermetic arts (astrology, tarot, geomancy, and the various branches of ceremonial magick) are constructed. The tarot is
a visual representation of qabalistic fundamentals and is the common denominator between the various Hermetic arts. One could
even say the tarot is the DNA of the Qabalah. Properly decoded it
reveals not only the mysteries of the Qabalah but also that of all
other Qabalah-based systems.

---

1. Let me assure the reader that my use of the word "creation" does not
imply that I subscribe in any way to a belief in an anthropomorphic "creator" or the absurd fairy tale that is the literal interpretation of the creation
myth of *Genesis*. By using the words "creation" and "creator," I am refer-
ring only to the ongoing process of the involving/evolving universe and the
transcendent force which drives that process.

2. QBL (קבל), Hebrew for "to receive." The Qabalah is not a book, but
an art and science of spiritual discovery. There are many qabalistic texts
and commentaries, but for the purpose of this book we will deal generally
with the fundamentals of the two branches of Hebrew mysticism known as
Maaseh Bereshith (History of Creation), of which the Sepher Yetzirah
(*Book of Formations*) forms the centerpiece; and *Masseh Merkabah* (History
of the Divine Throne or Chariot).

The *Tarot of Ceremonial Magick* does not announce any new discoveries or revelations. All the information incorporated in the cards and discussed in this book has been available for years to the diligent student fortunate enough to posses an extensive occult library and the considerable time and direction necessary to correlate, memorize, and digest the material. What I have simply done is to place pertinent data relating to astrology and the two most widely practiced varieties of Qabalah-based magick, (Enochian magick and Goetic evocation) upon the appropriate tarot cards themselves. This offers the opportunity for the student to painlessly absorb large amounts of technical and symbolic information simply by working with the cards.

As far as the images on the cards are concerned, I have not been so presumptuous as to stray too far from the traditional archetypes. The cards are unique, not because of the novelty of the artwork and images, but because of the traditional magical collateral material. It is not my intention to lure you away from any tarot deck you may currently prefer, but to help you understand the incalculable power and significance of whatever deck you may be using.

While it is relatively easy to find someone who is knowledgeable concerning the occult arts, it is very rare indeed to meet someone who actually practices them. For the theorist, I am confident that the *Tarot of Ceremonial Magick* will prove fascinating and informative; but for practitioners of ceremonial magick, I have no doubt that it will be welcomed as a useful and formidable addition to their magical arsenal.

CHAPTER ONE

The Qabalistic Mandala

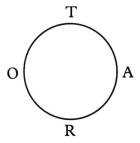

The traditional version of the *Wheel of Fortune* card displays four
letters, T A R O placed upon the rim of a great wheel. As the wheel
turns we read the letters in a variety of orders and permutations
including: OTAR (to purify oneself), ROTA (the wheel), AROT (vig-
ilance), TORA (the Law), ORAT (awe), TROA (gate), AT OR (thou
art), RATOT (vibration)

A little imagination and a free afternoon with a Hebrew and
Latin lexicon will render a dizzying array of other meanings and
messages. My point is more fundamental. The tarot is a wheel, a
mandala revealing the mechanics of creation. Each card has its
place upon the great wheel, from the inscrutable Zero of the *Fool*
to the dense materiality of the *Ten of Disks*. For our study we will
move from the center of the wheel outwards; from the cosmic to
the mundane. As we approach the rim of the wheel we will begin
to recognize aspects of our own being and of the world around us.

Used with skill, the tarot allows us to observe this development so we may trace the hidden influences that underlie and support our world and our being.

In order for the tarot to speak to us we must first learn its language—a language of numbers, of colors, of images. We must also try to understand the fundamentals of the spiritual discipline that created that language, the Holy Qabalah.

ONE & FOUR—A RULE OF THUMB

> *"And the Elohim created Ath-h-ADAM: in the image of the Elohim created They them; male and female created They them."* Genesis I:27

If we could for a moment put ourselves in the place of the early Hebrew mystics and view the above verse from the first book of Moses with the same holy awe as did they, we would begin our investigation of deity by first investigating ourselves.

Even before birth, the child in the womb finds its thumb and recognizes this digit as a source of comfort and self nurturing. It is the thumb's opposition to the other four fingers that first enabled the human hand to make tools, weapons, and fire. The hand distinguishes primates and humankind from the rest of the animal kingdom and is an appropriate symbol of the dominion of the human race. For this reason it is safe to assume that the hand was a fundamental subject of speculation and meditation among the ancient qabalists.

The qabalists teach that the Hebrew alphabet is the very tool of creation, taught by God to the angels and by the angels to Adam. The Hebrew word for hand is Yod ‘ (YVD), the tenth letter of the Hebrew alphabet, and represents numerically the number ten. Interestingly enough the remaining twenty-one Hebrew letters are variations of the letter Yod. Yod could indeed be called the source of all the letters.

Because the human hand has four fingers and one thumb which vivifies them (four ruled by a fifth), the ancient qabalists surmised that the "hand" of the Creator (the mechanics of the involving/evolving universe) must be an absolute unity which manifests through a fourfold process. This formula is universal and permeates all levels of existence and consciousness. To express the mechanics of this very fundamental observation, the Hebrew mystics embodied the formula in the concept of single God with a four letter name, יהוה IHVH.[1]

JEHOVAH IS A FOUR-LETTER WORD

These four letters, יהוה, are representative of four descending worlds through which the creative process is actualized:

י **Atziluth**, the Archetypal World, is the highest and most perfect of the four worlds. In Atziluth the male and female aspects of deity are united in bliss. The remaining three worlds are the product of this union, and continue to diminish in purity. Atziluth could be considered the *will* of deity in its purest aspect.

ה **Briah** is the Creative World in which the pure light of Atziluth begins to become organized. This is the throne and abode of the highest Angels and could be viewed as the *heart* of deity.

ו **Yetzirah** is the World of Formation where the universal organization of Briah becomes specific and a hierarchy of Angels with individual duties is established; the *mind* of deity.

ה (final) **Assiah** is the Material World, in which the impurities produced by the degeneration of the original light as it passes through the various worlds is crystalized to form the material world, nature, and human existence.

The world of Assiah is also the abode of the qliphoth, the shells or receptacles which in the three higher worlds serve to hold the divine light as it descends, but after serving their purpose are cast down like burned-out light bulbs into Assiah. These shells, made up of the grosser elements of the three higher worlds, still contain

---

1. Hebrew is written from right to left. י I (Yod), ה H (Heh), ו V (Vav), ה H (Heh). יהוה is commonly pronounced Jehovah; this ineffable Name of God was intoned only once a year by the High Priest of Israel in the Holy of Holies. The correct pronunciation of this word remains the most closely guarded secret of esoteric Judaism. When reading from the Scriptures, pious Jews say instead the substitute name "Adonai."

enough vivifying force to make them troublesome. Not spirits in the true sense of the term, these vessels aimlessly seek in vain to refill themselves with the living light. However, because in their new environment of Assiah the light does not exist in the rarified states as in the higher worlds, the qliphoth are cut off from the pure energy and become as it were wandering vacuums which seek to suck as much of the essence of the light as they can from the native inhabitants of Assiah (including humans).

Armed with this understanding we can now see why the qliphoth manifest the averse qualities of their original homes in the three higher worlds. Thus, that which once held the pure essence of the *unity* of the universe (Kether) now manifests as Thaumiel (Twins of God); the *harmony* of the sixth Sephira Tiphareth becomes the qliphoth known as Thagirion (the Litigation).

It must be remembered that the qliphoth are a natural and necessary part of the nature of deity as envisioned by the qabalists. Like the Titans of Greek mythology and the Giants of the *Nibelungenlied*, the qliphoth do the dirty work of building and supporting the material world as we perceive it. They are dangerous to us only when ungoverned, unrecognized or ignored. In fact, much of what we ignorantly believe to be ourselves (*i.e.*, our bodies, minds, personalities) can be considered qliphotic containers for the incomprehensibly subtle essence that is our true identity.

The four qabalistic worlds also serve as the blueprints for the four parts of the human soul, known in the Qabalah as *Chiah*, the life force; *Neschamah*, the divine soul-intuition; *Ruach*, the intellect; and *Nephesh*, the animal soul. They are also exemplified in the four primal Elements of the antiquity, Fire, Water, Air, and Earth respectively. As we will see, these worlds and these Elements are represented in the Tarot by the four suits, Wands-Fire-Atziluth; Cups-Water-Briah; Swords-Air-Yetzirah; and Disks-Earth-Assiah. This four-fold division is further extended within each Tarot suit and expressed in the Court Cards. The Knights[2]

---

2. Titles of the Court Cards vary according to tradition and antiquity. They include: King, Queen, Knight and Page (or Squire); King, Queen, Prince and Princess. The *Tarot of Ceremonial Magick* uses the same titles as Crowley's Thoth deck: Knight, Queen, Prince and Princess.

represent the fiery aspect of their respective suits, the Queens the watery, the Princes the airy, and the Princesses the earthy. But more on this later.

TEN & TWENTY TWO

The Thirty-Two Mysterious Paths of Wisdom

It is a basic technique of the qabalist to search for hidden meanings of significant words and numbers by dissecting them and examining their components. To delve deeper into the mysteries of four we discover that it is defined in more detail by other numbers:

0 + (or –) 4 (indicating that four, and indeed all numbers, somehow came out of zero);
1 + 3 (revealing the mystery that one can only be adequately defined by three correlatives);
2 + 2 (suggesting that the initial act of creation was an act of reflection).

Most interesting of all is to look at four as a progression of 0 + 1 + 2 + 3 + 4. Here we see four as a developmental process, and the resulting sum = 10 = Yod (Hebrew for the "hand"), the fundamental divine letter. Four conceals and defines ten and *vice versa*.

Ten is obviously a very important qabalistic number. We will see it graphically expressed in the ten emanations (Sephiroth) of the Tree of Life,[3] and in the Small Cards of the tarot, Ace through Ten, (a set of ten for each of the four suits). The Tree of Life is a map of the universe, and is the fundamental qabalistic diagram. It illustrates the tenfold process of the descent of Godhead into matter (humanity), and the twenty-two step process of our return back. So important is the Tree of Life to our understanding of the qabalistic principles of the tarot, that I will take just a moment to introduce the fundamentals of its construction. I hope the qabalistic purist will forgive the crudeness of the following anecdote.

---

3. See the Tree of Life on page 12.

Imagine, if you can, the lonely predicament of the Absolute.[4]

So perfect is the oneness of the Absolute that there is no way for It to examine Its own infinitude. Why It should desire to do so is beyond our comprehension, but tradition maintains that the impulse to create drives the One to seek self-examination. But how is this done? There is no "outside" of an infinite One. It cannot hold a mirror up and look at Itself. Yet It can reflect Itself by turning Its attention inward in just the same way a yogi closes his eyes and turns his or her attention inward in meditation until consciousness reaches the perfect center of being. This perfect inward reflection allows the One to recognize the conditions of Its oneness, but by doing so creates a second condition (One and Its reflection).

This realization of Self instantly brings with it a third condition, for no sooner does the Self realize what It is, it also realizes what It is not. In other words, we have the Self (1), the reflection, or Not-Self (2), and the knowledge they are not the same thing (3).

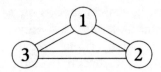

---

4. We will ignore, for the purpose of this brief and extremely inadequate discussion, the abstract concepts of the three varieties of qabalistic "Nothing" from which the Absolute proceeded: Ain (Nothing), Ain Soph (Without Limit), and Ain Soph Aur (Limitless Light).

This may seem very abstract, but even the exoteric branches of the world's great religions acknowledge in some way this threefold view of absolute unity. Brahma-Vishnu-Shiva; Father-Son-Holy Spirit, all echo the mechanics of this Supernal Triad.

Now we must view the trinity of 1-2-3 as the primal unit. The same impulse that made 1 reflect to realize 2, now impels the Supernal Triad to do the same;

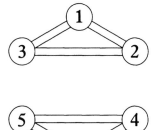

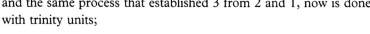

and the same process that established 3 from 2 and 1, now is done with trinity units;

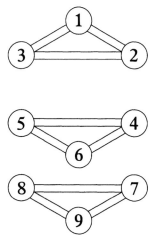

Finally the whole process attempts to repeat itself by the establishment of a single unit (10); a reflection of a reflection (9) of a reflection (6) of the Absolute (1).

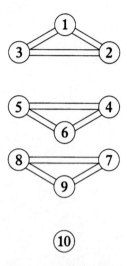

This assembly of ten Sephiroth is joined by twenty-two paths, forming the complete diagram known as the Tree of Life.

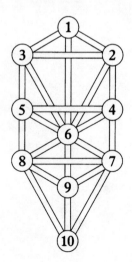

The top Sephira[5] is called Kether, the Crown. Two is Chokmah, Wisdom. Three is Binah, Understanding. Four is Chesed, Mercy. Five is Geburah, Strength. Six is Tiphareth, Beauty. Seven is Netzach, Victory. Eight is Hod, Splendor. Nine is Yesod, the Foundation. Ten is Malkuth, the Kingdom.

Perhaps the most concise and profound elucidation of the above process was written by Aleister Crowley and included in his classic text on the tarot, *The Book of Thoth*.[6]

The Naples Arrangement

$61 = 0$.

$61 + 146 = 0$ as Undefined (Space).

$61 + 146 + 207 = 0$ as basis of Possible Vibration.[7]

1. The Point: Positive yet indefinable,
2. The Point: Distinguishable from 1 other.
3. The Point: Defined by relation to 2 others.
     The Abyss—between Ideal and Actual.
4. The Point: Defined by 3 co-ordinates: Matter.
5. Motion (Time)—Heh, the Womb; for only through Motion and in Time can events occur.
6. The Point: now self-conscious because able to define itself in terms of above.
7. The Point's Idea of Bliss (Ananda).
8. The Point's Idea of Thought (Chit).
9. The Point's Idea of Being (Sat).
10. The Point's Idea of Itself fulfilled in its complement, as determined by 7, 8 and 9.

Each of the four qabalistic worlds is represented by its own Tree of Life through which flows the pure energy of the Absolute. Each Sephira, and each Tree of Life, receives the energy from the one above it and transmits it to the one below. The lower the power descends, the more diluted and polluted the energy becomes. The

---

5. Sephira (singular), Sephiroth (plural).
6. Aleister Crowley, *The Book of Thoth* (York Beach, ME: Samuel Weiser, 1991), p. 32.
7. $61 = $Ain; $61 + 146 = $Ain Soph; $61 + 146 + 207 = $Ain Soph Aur. The three veils of the Negative preceding One.

ten Sephiroth of Atziluth, for example, are very close to the source and are therefore very pure. They are the abodes of the ten aspects of Deity represented by the great *Divine Names*. These *Divine Names* rule the *Archangels* who reside in the next lower world, Briah, who in turn rule the *Angels* in the next lower world, Yetzirah, who in turn rule the planetary intelligences of the lowest world, *Assiah*.

In the world of Assiah, Kether (1) is the Sphere of the Primum Mobile. Chokmah (2) is the Sphere of the Zodiac or fixed Stars. Binah (3) is the Sphere of Saturn; Chesed (4) is the Sphere of Jupiter; Geburah (5) is the Sphere of Mars; Tiphareth (6) is the Sphere of the Sun; Netzach (7) is the Sphere of Venus; Hod (8) is the Sphere of Mercury; Yesod (9) is the Sphere of the Moon; and Malkuth (10) is the Sphere of the Elements. I'll talk more on the Tree of Life in the next chapter.

Continuing our qabalistic examination of human body we of course observe a total of ten fingers and ten toes = 20. If we spell the Hebrew letter Yod in full (YVD) it enumerates to twenty,[8] reaffirming the direct relationship between ten and twenty. We can be certain that such coincidences did not go unnoticed by the qabalistic pioneers.

Finally, between the ten fingers is another part of the human body which is instrumental in separating us from the beasts, the tongue—the organ of speech, and between the ten toes is found that which makes each of us a creative "god," the penis or vagina. In all, twenty-two fundamental landmarks of the human body. Throughout our study of the tarot we will not stray very far from Four, Ten, and Twenty-Two, for it is upon these numbers that the mandala of the tarot is built. It is these numbers that turn the great wheel.

---

8. Yod = 10, Vav = 6, Daleth = 4.

CHAPTER TWO

The Twenty-Two Trumps

The 78 cards of the tarot are divided into four categories:

- 22 Trumps
- 4 Aces
- 16 Court Cards
- 36 Small Cards.

It is no coincidence that there are twenty-two letters in the sacred Hebrew alphabet (affirming the qabalist's awful respect for *Genesis* I:27), and these twenty-two letters are expressed in the tarot as the twenty-two Trumps.[1] The common titles of the Trumps are: Fool, Magician, High Priestess, Empress, Emperor, Hierophant, Lovers, Chariot, Justice, Hermit, Wheel of Fortune, Strength, Hanged Man, Death, Temperance, Devil, Tower, Star, Moon, Sun, Judgement, and the World.[2]

The Trumps each have their place upon the Tree of Life and serve as the paths which connect the ten Sephiroth. It is said that the universe was created by a lightning flash that descended the ten Sephiroth of the Tree of Life from top to bottom. The path of humanity's return to Godhead, however, is by way of the twenty-two Paths, which start at the bottom and climb like a serpent up the Tree.

---

1. The Trumps are often referred to as the Atus of Tahuti ("Houses" of the Egyptian God, Thoth).
2. The Trumps of the *Tarot of Ceremonial Magick* vary little from the traditional titles. Following the precedent set in Crowley's Thoth deck, the Magician is **Magus**, Strength is **Lust**, the Wheel of Fortune is **Fortune**, Temperance is **Art**, Judgement is **Æon**, and the World is **Universe**.

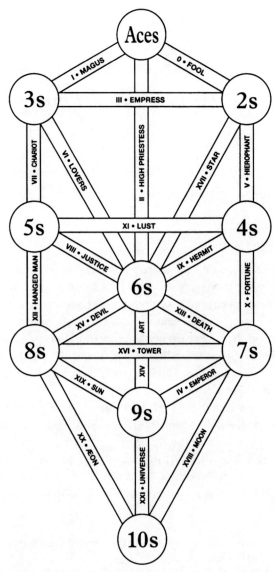

Figure 1. Placement of the 22 Trumps upon the Paths of the Tree of Life.

THE 22 LETTERS OF
THE HEBREW ALPHABET

The Hebrew alphabet is divided into three categories;

3 Mother letters (Aleph א , Mem מ , Shin ש);

7 Double letters (Beth ב, Gimel ג, Daleth ד, Kaph כ, Pe פ, Resh ר, and Tav ת); and

12 Simple letters (Heh ה, Vav ו, Zain ז, Cheth ח, Teth ט, Yod י, Lamed ל, Nun נ, Samekh ס, Ayin ע, Tzaddi צ, and Qoph ק.

The division of the twenty-two letters into three–seven–twelve was not an arbitrary act by our qabalistic ancestors. It was based upon a simple yet profound attempt to reenact the creation of the dimensional universe. In a sense, this reeactment is the exact opposite of the above meditation by which we created the Tree of Life, yet the results are profoundly similar. Please bear with me for one more imaginary projection into the mind of God.

Imagine, if you can, that you are the deity and you have not yet begun to create the universe. You are alone. There is no *outside* of you. You are just you; the One; the Only; the Singularity. For some reason, perhaps out of boredom, you decide to create the universe. But because there is as yet no outside of you in which to do this, you must first give yourself some elbow room. And so you reach straight up and establish infinite HEIGHT. As you do this the dimension of Height is sealed and begins to expand in never-ending concentric wavelets.

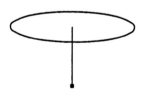

Figure 2. Height.

Next you reach straight down and do the same thing with the infinite DEPTH.

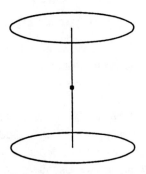

*Figure 3. Mother Letter ℵ Aleph, represents the
dimension of Height-Depth.*

The HEIGHT–DEPTH line is the first dimension and is represented
by the first Mother letter of the sacred Hebrew alphabet, ℵ, Aleph.

Next you reach to the right[3] and seal the infinite SOUTH, then
to the left and seal the infinite NORTH.

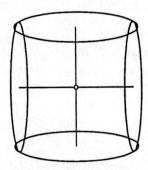

*Figure 4. Mother Letter ש Shin, represents the
dimension of South-North.*

The SOUTH–NORTH line is the second dimension and is represented by the Mother letter, Shin.

---

3. For reference we must assume you are facing some direction, so let's
say you are facing East.

Next you reach forward and seal the infinite EAST, then in back of you and seal the infinite WEST.

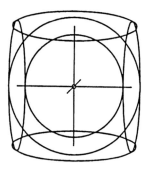

*Figure 5. Mother Letter ם Mem, represents
the dimension of East-West.*

The EAST–WEST line is the third dimension and is represented by the Mother letter, Mem.

Through these three sealed dimensions (the three Mother letters) all subsequent aspects of the Universe were created. Because the seals of Height–Depth, South–North, East–West are eternally expanding, they perpetually intersect and in doing so form a cube.[4]

The cube's center and six faces are represented by the seven Double Letters of the Hebrew alphabet: Center—ת Tav; Top—ב Beth; Bottom—ג Gimel; South—ר Resh; North—פ Pe; East—ד Daleth; West—כ Kaph.

The twelve edges of the cube are represented by the twelve Simple Letters: Northeast—ה Heh; Southeast—ו Vav; East-above—ז Zain; East-below—ח Cheth; North-above—ט Teth; North-below—י Yod; Northwest—ל Lamed; Southwest—נ Nun;

---

4. You may protest that this story is a pitifully inadequate attempt to dimensionalize a transdimensional process. To this the qabalist will wholeheartedly agree, adding that "dimensionalizing the transdimensional" is a perfect description of creation.

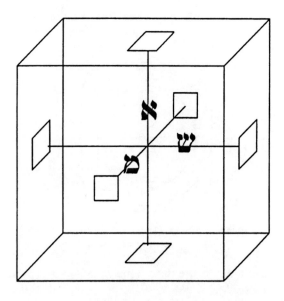

Figure 6. Cube showing intersection of dimensions.

West-above—ס Samekh; West-below—ע Ayin; South-above—צ Tzaddi; South-below—ק Qoph.

It is easy to understand why the qabalists consider the Hebrew alphabet to be the very tool of creation.

THE 22 TAROT TRUMPS

The twenty-two Tarot Trumps are divided into the same three categories as the Hebrew alphabet:

3 Mother Letters = 3 Primitive Elements:

Air   (**Fool**—Aleph)
Water   (**Hanged Man**—Mem)
Fire   (**Æon**—Shin)

[Earth is represented by the Universe card which also represents the planet Saturn.]

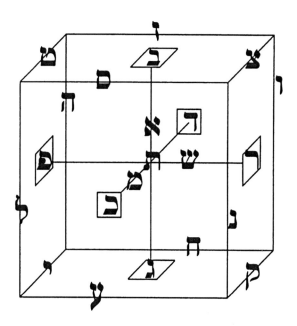

Figure 7. Qabalistic Cube.

7 Double Letters = 7 Planets:

Mercury	(**Magus**—Beth)
Moon	(**High Priestess**—Gimel)
Venus	(**Empress**—Daleth)
Jupiter	(**Fortune**—Kaph)
Mars	(**Tower**—Pe)
Sun	(**Sun**—Resh)
Saturn	(**Universe**—Tav)

12 Simple Letters = 12 Signs of the Zodiac:

Aries	(**Emperor**—Tzaddi)	Libra	(**Justice**—Lamed)
Taurus	(**Hierophant**—Vav)	Scorpio	(**Death**—Nun)
Gemini	(**Lovers**—Zain)	Sagittarius	(**Art**—Samekh)
Cancer	(**Chariot**—Cheth)	Capricorn	(**Devil**—Ayin)
Leo	(**Lust**—Teth)	Aquarius	(**Star**—Heh)
Virgo	(**Hermit**—Yod)	Pisces	(**Moon**—Qoph)

The Trumps are above, and quite apart from, the other cards in the deck. They are representative of very fundamental cosmic principles which infinitely transcend their zodiacal, planetary, or elemental attributions. Each Trump exercises its unique nature from the highest heavens to the lowest abodes of the qliphoth and merit the highest level of spiritual respect. A majority of Trumps in a tarot reading generally indicates forces beyond the control of the questioner.

In addition to the above elemental, planetary, and zodiacal information, the Trumps of the *Tarot of Ceremonial Magick* also display the magical seals of the geniis of the Domarum Mercurii (House of Mercury), found on the bottom left of each Trump; and the geniis of the Carcerorum Qliphoth (Prison of the Shells), displayed on the bottom right. These pairs of spirits were first revealed in 1912 in Aleister Crowley's *Liber Arcanorum τῶν ATU τοῦ Tahuti Quas Vidit Asar in Amennti Sub Figura CCXXXI. Liber Carcerorum τῶν Qliphoth cum suis Geniis. Adduntur Sigilla et Nomina Eorum.*[5] Very little is known about the circumstances under which Crowley received these symbols, but it is clear that they provide for the first time the names and sigils of spirits that are specifically unique to each of the twenty-two Atus or Tarot Trumps. Most notable to the Magician are the titles of the abodes of these geniis; the "*House* of Mercury" and the "*Prison* of Shells." The former indicating each Trump's representitive agent of transmission, the later providing the key which can "lock up" the troublesome or destructive opposition to that transmission. Together these symbols demonstrate the entire magical spectrum of influence represented by the card—the genii of the Atu standing guard over the prison of the qliphoth.

---

5. Aleister Crowley, "The Book of the Secrets of the Atu of Tahuti, which Asar saw in Amenti (under the number 231). The Book of the Prison of the Qliphoth with their Geniis, their symbols and names are added." *The Equinox* I(8) (York Beach, ME: Samuel Weiser, 1992), p. 197, and Appendix Five of this book.

The descriptive page facing the illustration of each card contains itemized information concerning the card, including general divinatory meanings and additional data not found on the cards themselves. At the bottom of each text page for the Trumps is a small two-line poem taken from Aleister Crowley's *The Book of Thoth*, p. 219, "The Atu: Mnemonics."

KEY 0

Fool

Spirit of the Æther

AIR

General divinatory meanings:

> *In spiritual matters:* The beginning of the Great Work. Divine innocence. Foolishness is holiness. The Holy Ghost descends when opposites are balanced.

> *In matters of the heart:* A fool for love. A stranger competes publicly for the hand of the beloved.

> *In intellectual matters:* Divine madness. Reason is transcended.

> *In material matters:* Folly. Gain or loss through foolish action.

Hebrew Letter: א Aleph   **Numerical Value:** 1

English Equivalent: A   **Meaning:** An ox

Colors: Bright pale yellow, Sky blue, Blue emerald green, Emerald flecked gold.

Path of the Sepher Yetzirah: Scintillating Intelligence.

Traditional Image: A bearded Ancient seen in profile.

Mercurial Genii: A(ע)u-iao-u(ע)a

Qliphothic Genii: Amprodias

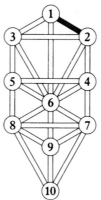

Crowley's Mnemonic:

> Truth, laughter, lust: Wine's Holy Fool! Veil rent,
> Lewd madness is sublime enlightenment.

KEY I

Magus

Magus of Power

MERCURY

General divinatory meanings:

In spiritual matters: Unconscious will. The process of continuous creation.

In matters of the heart: Ambiguity. Deception. All things may not be as they appear.

In intellectual matters: Concentration. Meditation. The mind is used to direct the will.

In material matters: Manipulation. Communication. The guileful maneuverings of a business transaction.

Hebrew Letter: ב Beth   **Numerical Value:** 2

English Equivalent: B   **Meaning:** House

Colors: Yellow, Purple, Grey, Indigo rayed violet.

Path of the Sepher Yetzirah: Intelligence of Transparency.

Traditional Image: A fair youth with winged helmet and heels, equipped as a Magician, displays his art.

Mercurial Genii: Be(ע)θaoooabitom

Qliphothic Genii: Baratchial

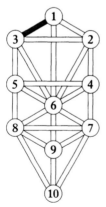

Crowley's Mnemonic:

> The Word of Wisdom weaves the web of lies,
> Weds irreducible Infinities.

KEY II

High Priestess

Priestess of the Silver Star

MOON

General divinatory meanings:

In spiritual matters: Symbol of the highest initiation. The link
between the archetypal and formative worlds.

In matters of the heart: An Initiatrix. Wooing by enchantment.

In intellectual matters: The idea behind the form. Possibility.

In material matters: Fluctuation. Change. Time may not be
right for decision concerning mundane affairs.

Hebrew Letter: ג Gimel   **Numerical Value:** 3

English Equivalent: G   **Meaning:** Camel

Colors: Blue, Silver, Cold pale blue, Silver rayed sky blue.

Path of the Sepher Yetzirah: Uniting Intelligence.

Traditional Image: A crowned priestess sits before the veil of Isis
between the pillars of Seth.

Mercurial Genii: Giωnosapφωllois

Qliphothic Genii: Gargophias

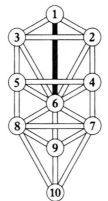

Crowley's Mnemonic:

Mother, moon-maiden, playmate, bride of Pan;
God's Angel-Minister to every man.

KEY III

Empress

Daughter of the Mighty Ones

VENUS

General divinatory meanings:

In spiritual matters: The Holy Graal. Love unites the will.

In matters of the heart: Love. Beauty. Friendship. Success. Romance.

In intellectual matters: Passive balance. The feminine point of view.

In material matters: The door is open. Disregard the details and concentrate on the big picture.

Hebrew Letter: ד Daleth   **Numerical Value:** 4

English Equivalent: D   **Meaning:** Door

Colors: Emerald green, Sky blue, Early spring green, Bright rose rayed pale green.

Path of the Sepher Yetzirah: Illuminating Intelligence.

Traditional Image: Crowned with stars, a winged goddess stands upon the moon.

Mercurial Genii: Dηa(st)artarωθ

Qliphothic Genii: Dagdagiel

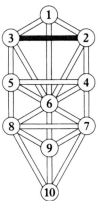

Crowley's Mnemonic:

Beauty, display thine Empire! Truth above
Thought's reach: the wholeness of the world is Love.

KEY IV

Emperor

Sun of the Morning, Chief among the Mighty

ARIES

(March 21 to April 20)

Fire Sign (Cardinal)

Ruler: Mars   **Exalted Planet:** Sun

General divinatory meanings:

In spiritual matters: Creative wisdom radiating upon the organized man or woman.

In matters of the heart: Domination after conquest. Quarrelsomeness. Paternal love.

In intellectual matters: Ambition. Thought ruled by creative, masculine, fiery energy. Stubbornness.

In material matters: War. Authority. Energy in its most temporal form. Swift, impermanent action. Overconfidence.

Hebrew Letter: צ Tzaddi   **Numerical Value:** 90

English Equivalent: Tz, X   **Meaning:** Fish hook

Colors: Scarlet, Red, Brilliant flame, Glowing red.

Path of the Sepher Yetzirah: Natural Intelligence.

Traditional Image: A flame-clad god bearing equivalent symbols.

Mercurial Genii: Xanθa(st)eran(shq)i(st)

Qliphothic Genii: Tzuflifu

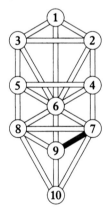

Crowley's Mnemonic:

Sire and inceptor, Emperor and King
Of all things mortal, hail Him lord of Spring!

KEY V

Hierophant

Magus of the Eternal

TAURUS

(April 21 to May 20)

Earth Sign (Fixed)

Ruler: Venus   **Exalted Planet:** Moon

General divinatory meanings:

> *In spiritual matters:* The Holy Guardian Angel. The uniting of that which is above with that which is below.

> *In matters of the heart:* Love is indicated, but the nature of that love is yet to be revealed.

> *In intellectual matters:* Inspiration. Teaching. Organization. Discipline.

> *In material matters:* Strength. Endurance. Toil. Help from superiors.

Hebrew Letter: ו Vav   **Numerical Value:** 6

English Equivalent: V, O, U   **Meaning:** Nail

Colors: Red-orange, Deep indigo, Deep warm olive, Rich brown.

Path of the Sepher Yetzirah: Triumphal or Eternal One.

Traditional Image: Between the pillars sits an Ancient.

Mercurial Genii: Vuaretza-(a secret name follows)

Qliphothic Genii: Uriens

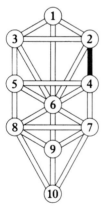

Crowley's Mnemonic:

> Wisdom to each apportioned to his want
> By modes of Light, shed forth, great Hierophant!

KEY VI

Lovers

Children of the Voice;
Oracle of the Mighty Gods

GEMINI

(May 21 to June 20)

Air Sign (Mutable)

Ruler: Mercury

General divinatory meanings:

> *In spiritual matters:* Intuition. Be open to your own inner voice.
>
> *In matters of the heart:* A well-intended, arranged marriage. An artificial union.
>
> *In intellectual matters:* Analysis followed by synthesis.
>
> *In material matters:* Indecision. Instability. Superficiality.

Hebrew Letter: ז Zain   **Numerical Value:** 7

English Equivalent: Z   **Meaning:** Sword

Colors: Orange, Pale mauve, New yellow leather, Reddish grey.

Path of the Sepher Yetzirah: Disposing One.

Traditional Image: A prophet, young, and in the Sign of Osiris Risen.

Mercurial Genii: Zooωasar

Qliphothic Genii: Zamradiel

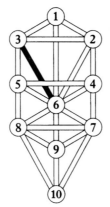

Crowley's Mnemonic:

> To each his Understanding sooth discovers
> Wordless: your mode, immortal Twins and Lovers!

KEY VII

Chariot

Child of the Powers of the Waters;
Lord of the Triumph of Light

CANCER

(June 21 to July 21)

Water Sign (Cardinal)

Ruler: Moon   **Exalted Planet:** Jupiter

General divinatory meanings:

In spiritual matters: Light in the Darkness. The burden you carry may be the Holy Graal.

In matters of the heart: Faithfulness. Hope. Obedience. A protective relationship.

In intellectual matters: Firm, even violent adherence to dogma or tradition.

In material matters: Victory. Triumph. Chain of command.

Hebrew Letter: ח Cheth   **Numerical Value:** 8

English Equivalent: C, Ch   **Meaning:** Fence

Colors: Amber, Maroon, Rich bright russet, Dark greenish brown.

Path of the Sepher Yetzirah: Intelligence of the House of Influence.

Traditional Image: A young and holy king under the starry canopy.

Mercurial Genii: Chiva-abrahadabra-cadaxviii

Qliphothic Genii: Characith

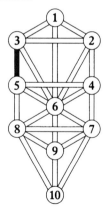

Crowley's Mnemonic:

Behold the Chariot! Through the water floods
The Sangraal, life and rapture, Wine's and Blood's!

KEY VIII

Justice

Daughter of the Lords of Truth;
Ruler of the Balance

LIBRA

(Sept. 23 to Oct. 22)

Air Sign (Cardinal)

Ruler: Venus   **Exalted Planet:** Saturn

General divinatory meanings:

> *In spiritual matters:* Equilibrium. Karmic law. The dance of life. All possibilities.

> *In matters of the heart:* A woman satisfied.

> *In intellectual matters:* Balance. Weigh each thought against its opposite.

> *In material matters:* Lawsuits. Treaties. Pause and look before you leap.

Hebrew Letter: ל Lamed   **Numerical Value:** 30

English Equivalent: L   **Meaning:** Ox goad

Colors: Emerald green, Blue, Deep blue-green, Pale green.

Path of the Sepher Yetzirah: Faithful Intelligence.

Traditional Image: A conventional figure of Justice with scales and balances.

Mercurial Genii: Lusanaherandraton

Qliphothic Genii: Lafcursiax

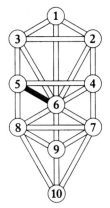

Crowley's Mnemonic:

> Adjustment! Rhythm writhes through every act.
> Wild is the dance; its balance is exact.

KEY IX

Hermit

Prophet of the Eternal;
Magus of the Voice of Power

VIRGO

(Aug. 23 to Sept. 22)

Earth Sign (Mutable)

Ruler: Mercury   **Exalted Planet:** Mercury

General divinatory meanings:

In spiritual matters: Divine seed of all things. By silence comes inspiration & wisdom.

In matters of the heart: Wandering alone. Temporary solitude.

In intellectual matters: Creative contemplation.

In material matters: A virgin. Retirement from involvement in current events.

Hebrew Letter: ' Yod   **Numerical Value:** 10

English Equivalent: Y, I, J   **Meaning:** Hand

Colors: Yellowish green, Slate grey, Green grey, Plum.

Path of the Sepher Yetzirah: Intelligence of Will.

Traditional Image: Wrapped in a cloak and cowl, an Ancient walketh, bearing a lamp and staff.

Mercurial Genii: Iehuvaha(st)an($\mathfrak{Y}$)θatan

Qliphothic Genii: Yamatu

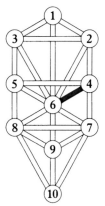

Crowley's Mnemonic:

Most secret seed of all Life's serpent plan,
Virgin, the Hermit goes, dumb Guardian.

KEY X

Fortune

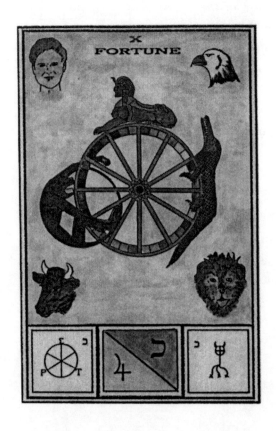

Lord of the Forces of Life

JUPITER

General divinatory meanings:

> *In spiritual matters:* Continual change. In the midst of revolving phenomena reach joyously the motionless center.
>
> *In matters of the heart:* Carefree love, wanton pleasure.
>
> *In intellectual matters:* Amusement. Fun.
>
> *In material matters:* Change of fortune, usually good.

Hebrew Letter: ‎כ Kaph   **Numerical Value:** 20

English Equivalent: K   **Meaning:** Closed hand

Colors: Violet, Blue, Rich purple, Bright blue rayed yellow.

Path of the Sepher Yetzirah: Intelligence of Conciliation.

Traditional Image: A wheel of six shafts, whereon revolve the Triad of Hermanubis, Sphinx, and Typhon.

Mercurial Genii: Kerugunaviel

Qliphothic Genii: Kurgasiax

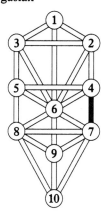

Crowley's Mnemonic:

> Sped by its energies triune, the Wheel
> Of Fortune spins: its Axle's immobile.

KEY XI

Lust

Daughter of the Flaming Sword

LEO

(July 22 to August 22)

Fire Sign (Fixed)

Ruler: Sun

General divinatory meanings:

> *In spiritual matters:* Understanding. The Will of the New Aeon.

> *In matters of the heart:* Passion. Sense smitten with ecstasy. Let love devour all.

> *In intellectual matters:* Energy independent of reason.

> *In material matters:* Strength. Courage. Utilization of magical power.

Hebrew Letter: ט Teth　　　　**Numerical Value:** 9

English Equivalent: T　　　　**Meaning:** Serpent

Colors: Greenish yellow, Deep purple, Grey, Reddish amber.

Path of the Sepher Yetzirah: Intelligence of all the Activities of the Spiritual Being.

Traditional Image: A smiling woman holds the open jaws of a fierce and powerful lion.

Mercurial Genii: Θal(ע)(st)er-a-dekerval

Qliphothic Genii: Temphioth

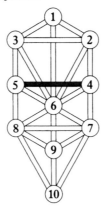

Crowley's Mnemonic:

> The Lion-Serpent begets Gods! Thy throne
> The rampant Beast, our Lady Babalon!

KEY XII

Hanged Man

Spirit of the Mighty Waters

WATER

General divinatory meanings:

> *In spiritual matters:* Redemption through sacrifice. Annihilation of Self in the Beloved.

> *In matters of the heart:* Martyrdom. Loss.

> *In intellectual matters:* Torment. Reversal.

> *In material matters:* Suspension. Death. Suffering.

Hebrew Letter: מ Mem   **Numerical Value:** 40

English Equivalent: M   **Meaning:** Water

Colors: Deep blue, Sea green, Deep olive green, White, flecked purple.

Path of the Sepher Yetzirah: Stable Intelligence.

Traditional Image: The figure of an hanged or crucified man.

Mercurial Genii: Malai

Qliphothic Genii: Malkunofat

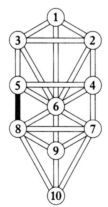

Crowley's Mnemonic:

> In Mother-Deeps of Ocean the God-Man
> Hangs, Lamp of the Abyss Æonian.

KEY XIII

Death

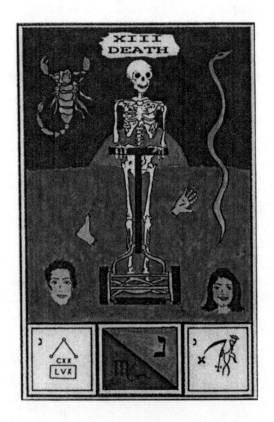

Children of the Great Transformers;
Lord of the Gate of Death

SCORPIO
(Oct. 23 to Nov. 22)

Water Sign (Fixed)

Ruler: Mars

General divinatory meanings:

In spiritual matters: End of a cycle. Transformation.

In matters of the heart: Raw sexuality. "Sex is death."

In intellectual matters: Stress becomes intolerable. Any change is welcome.

In material matters: Time. Age. Unexpected change. Death.

Hebrew Letter: ‎נ Nun   **Numerical Value:** 50

English Equivalent: N   **Meaning:** Fish

Colors: Green blue, Dull brown, Very dark brown, Livid indigo brown.

Path of the Sepher Yetzirah: Imaginative Intelligence.

Traditional Image: A skeleton with a Tau shaped scythe mowing men.

Mercurial Genii: Nadimraphoroioz(ע)θalai

Qliphothic Genii: Niantiel

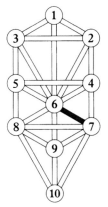

Crowley's Mnemonic:

Eagle, and Snake, and Scorpion! The Dance
Of Death whirls Life from Trance to Trance to Trance.

KEY XIV

Art

Daughter of the Reconcilers; Bringer-forth of Life

SAGITTARIUS

(Nov. 23 to Dec. 21)

Fire Sign (Mutable)

Ruler: Jupiter

General divinatory meanings:

> *In spiritual matters:* Transmutation through union of opposites.

> *In matters of the heart:* A perfect marriage exalts and transforms each partner.

> *In intellectual matters:* The scientific method.

> *In material matters:* Success follows complex manoeuvres.

Hebrew Letter: ס Samekh   **Numerical Value:** 60

English Equivalent: S   **Meaning:** Prop; tent pole

Colors: Blue, Yellow, Green, Dark vivid blue.

Path of the Sepher Yetzirah: Intelligence of Probation or Tentative One.

Traditional Image: The figure of Diana huntress.

Mercurial Genii: Salaθlala-amrodnaθ(ע)i(st)

Qliphothic Genii: Saksaksalim

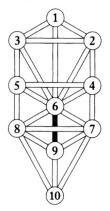

Crowley's Mnemonic:

> Solve, coagula! By V.I.T.R.I.O.L. shewn,
> The Tincture, the Elixir, and the Stone.

KEY XV

Devil

Lord of the Gates of Matter;
Child of the Forces of Time

CAPRICORN

(Dec. 22 to Jan. 19)

Earth Sign (Cardinal)

Ruler: Saturn   **Exalted Planet:** Mars

General divinatory meanings:

> *In spiritual matters:* "Thou hast no right but to do thy will."
>
> *In matters of the heart:* Obsession. Temptation. Ecstasy found in every phenomenon.
>
> *In intellectual matters:* Creative action, yet sublimely careless of result.
>
> *In material matters:* Unscrupulous ambition. Strength.

Hebrew Letter: ע Ayin   **Numerical Value:** 70

English Equivalent: O   **Meaning:** Eye

Colors: Indigo, Black, Blue black, Cold dark grey.

Path of the Sepher Yetzirah: Renovating Intelligence.

Traditional Image: The figure of Pan or Priapus.

Mercurial Genii: Oaoaaooo(ע)-i(st)

Qliphothic Genii: A'ano'nin

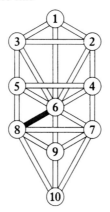

Crowley's Mnemonic:

> *Io Παν!* upon the summits the God-goat
> Leaps in wild lust of ecstasy afloat.

KEY XVI

Tower

Lord of the Hosts of the Mighty

MARS

General divinatory meanings:

In spiritual matters: Escape from the prison of organized life.

In matters of the heart: Renunciation of love. Quarreling.

In intellectual matters: Plans are destroyed.

In material matters: War. Danger. Sudden death.

Hebrew Letter: פ Pe   **Numerical Value:** 80

English Equivalent: P   **Meaning:** Mouth

Colors: Scarlet, Red, Venetian red, Bright red, rayed azure or emerald.

Path of the Sepher Yetzirah: Exciting Intelligence.

Traditional Image: A tower struck by forked lightning.

Mercurial Genii: Puraθmetai-apηmetai

Qliphothic Genii: Parfaxitas

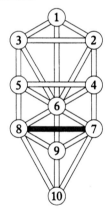

Crowley's Mnemonic:

Bellona, scream! Unhood the Hawks! The roar
Of Universes crashing into War!

KEY XVII

Star

Daughter of the Firmament;
Dweller between the Waters

AQUARIUS

(Jan. 20 to Feb. 18)

Air Sign (Fixed)

Ruler: Saturn

General divinatory meanings:

In spiritual matters: Clairvoyance. Visions. Dreams.

In matters of the heart: Hope. Love. Yearning.

In intellectual matters: Realization of inexhaustible possibilities. Dreaminess.

In material matters: Unexpected help. Renewal.

Hebrew Letter: ה Heh   **Numerical Value:** 5

English Equivalent: H   **Meaning:** Window

Colors: Violet, Sky blue, Bluish mauve, White, tinged purple.

Path of the Sepher Yetzirah: Natural Intelligence.

Traditional Image: The figure of a water-nymph disporting herself.

Mercurial Genii: Hoo-oorωi(st)

Qliphothic Genii: Hermethterith

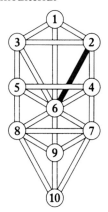

Crowley's Mnemonic:

Nuit, our Lady of the Stars! Event
Is all Thy play, sublime Experiment!

KEY XVIII

Moon

Ruler of Flux and Reflux;
Child of the Sons of the Mighty

PISCES

(Feb. 19 to March 20)

Water Sign (Mutable)

Ruler: Jupiter   **Exalted Planet:** Venus

General divinatory meanings:

In spiritual matters: The Dark Night of the Soul.

In matters of the heart: Deception. Falsehood.

In intellectual matters: Illusion. Madness.

In material matters: The threshold of significant change.

Hebrew Letter: ק Qoph   **Numerical Value:** 100

English Equivalent: Q   **Meaning:** Back of head

Colors: Crimson, Buff, flecked silver-white, Pinkish brown, Stone color.

Path of the Sepher Yetzirah: Corporeal Intelligence.

Traditional Image: The waning moon.

Mercurial Genii: Qani⊿nayx-ipamai

Qliphothic Genii: Qulielfi

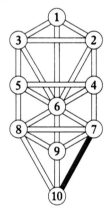

Crowley's Mnemonic:

> Witch-moon, upon thy beck of blood afloat
> The Midnight Beetle's brave prophetic Boat!

KEY XIX

Sun

Lord of the Fire of the World

SUN

General divinatory meanings:

> *In spiritual matters:* The Lord of the New Aeon. Spiritual emancipation.
>
> *In matters of the heart:* Pleasure. Shamelessness. Vanity.
>
> *In intellectual matters:* Frankness. Freedom brings sanity.
>
> *In material matters:* Glory. Riches. Enlightened civilization.

Hebrew Letter: ר Resh   **Numerical Value:** 200

English Equivalent: R   **Meaning:** Head or face

Colors: Orange, Gold yellow, Rich amber, Amber, rayed red.

Path of the Sepher Yetzirah: Collecting Intelligence.

Traditional Image: The Sun.

Mercurial Genii: Ra-a-gioselahladnaimawa-i(st)

Qliphothic Genii: Raflifu

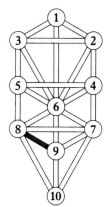

Crowley's Mnemonic:

> The Sun, our Father! Soul of Life and Light,
> Love and play freely, sacred in Thy sight!

KEY XX

Æon

Spirit of the Primal Fire

FIRE

General divinatory meanings:

In spiritual matters: Let every act be an act of worship.

In matters of the heart: Let every act be an act of love.

In intellectual matters: Final decision. Judgment.

In material matters: Learn from the past. Prepare for the future.

Hebrew Letter: ש Shin   **Numerical Value:** 300

English Equivalent: Sh   **Meaning:** Teeth

Colors: Orange scarlet, Vermillion, Scarlet flecked gold, Vermillion flecked crimson and emerald.

Path of the Sepher Yetzirah: Perpetual Intelligence.

Traditional Image: Israfel blowing the Last Trumpet. The dead arising from their tombs.

Mercurial Genii: Shabnax-odobor

Qliphothic Genii: Shalicu

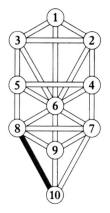

Crowley's Mnemonic:

Nuit, Hadit, Ra-Hoor-Khuit! The Aeon
Of the Twin Child! Exult, o Empyrean!

KEY XXI

Universe

Great One of the Night of Time

SATURN / EARTH

General divinatory meanings:

> *In spiritual matters:* Completion of the Great Work.
>
> *In matters of the heart:* Patience. Perseverance.
>
> *In intellectual matters:* Long, continued meditation.
>
> *In material matters:* Work accomplished. Reward. The end of the matter.

Hebrew Letter: ת Tav **Numerical Value:** 400

English Equivalent: Th **Meaning:** Cross

Colors: Indigo, Black, Blue black, Black flecked yellow.

Path of the Sepher Yetzirah: Administrative Intelligence.

Traditional Image: A demonstration of the Quadrature of the Circle.

Mercurial Genii: Thath'th'thith(ע)thuth-thi(st)

Qliphothic Genii: Thantifaxath

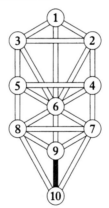

Crowley's Mnemonic:

> Naught becomes All to realise the span
> Of naught, O perfect Universe of Pan.

CHAPTER THREE

The Four Aces

After the Trumps, the remaining fifty-six cards are divided into four suits; Wands, Cups, Swords, and Disks. As mentioned earlier, these suits represent the four universal elements of Fire, Water, Air, and Earth respectively.

There is a fifth element, Spirit, which serves two most important functions:

(1) Spirit acts as a vibratory glue which bonds the other elements together in infinite combinations and proportions to form the phenomenal universe.

(2) Spirit also serves as the vibratory barrier between the bonded elements, keeping them separated just enough to assure their individual identity and purity. This active/passive nature makes Spirit the key element, for without Spirit all would be a chaotic soup.

So pervasive is Spirit's influence that it cannot be represented by a single tarot card or even a single suit. Instead, it reveals its presence and influence in the Aces and the Court Cards. This is exhibited perfectly in the Tablet of Union (Spirit Tablet) of the Enochian magical system of Dr. John Dee. As the *Tarot of Ceremonial Magick* incorporates a great deal of Enochian information on the cards, I will take a moment to review the basic principles of that system.[1]

---

1. Further insights into Enochian magick can be obtained by viewing my video, *Enochian Magick: The Art of Angelic Evolution* (Claremont, CA: Hooded Man Productions, 1994).

Between 1582 and 1589, the Elizabethan magus Dr. John Dee[2] and his clairvoyant colleague, Edward Kelley,[3] embarked upon one of the most remarkable magical adventures ever recorded.[4] It was Dee's consuming passion to speak directly with divine angelic beings in the same manner as the biblical patriarch, Enoch (hence the term "Enochian"). His motives were as much scientific as spiritual. He was, by all accounts, perhaps the most intelligent and knowledgeable man of his day. The world came to him for answers. Where then was he to turn for answers to the endless questions that haunted his insatiable curiosity, questions concerning life, science, nature and deity? To Dee it was only logical to attempt to access the very mind of God, and God's communicating angels, for more information and wisdom.

In the course of their invocations and ceremonially-induced visions, Dee and Kelley contacted numerous spirits who gave remarkably detailed instructions concerning the construction of various magical implements and furniture. Most significantly, they were taught an angelic language by which the spirits could be more easily invoked. The details of how this language was communicated are most complex, and have fascinated occult investigators for over 400 years. Suffice to say in this place that it is a true language with grammar and syntax, and the visionary experiences that are the result of properly intoning the various angelic "Calls"

---

2. 1527–1608. A true Renaissance magus, Dee was considered the greatest mind of his day and an "Ornament of the Age." Among other talents too numerous to mention here, he was the most celebrated mathematician of his day, and was the personal counselor to (and secret agent for) Queen Elizabeth I. For a more complete review of the achievements of this remarkable man, the reader is encouraged to read *John Dee—The World of an Elizabethan Magus* by Peter J. French (London: Routledge & Kegan Paul, 1972) and *Elizabethan Magic* by Robert Turner (London: Element Books, 1989).

3. Edward Kelley (sometimes spelled Kelly): 1555–1595.

4. See Meric Casaubon's *A True and Faithful Relation of what passed for many Yeers between Dr. John Dee ... and some Spirits* (London, 1659; reprinted New York: Magickal Childe, 1992).

continue to be a source of wonder and spiritual insight to modern magicians.

Dee took copious notes of the workings and much of the material has survived to this day. In the late 1800s Enochian magic became of special interest to S. L. MacGregor Mathers and the adepts of the Golden Dawn, who digested and synthesized much of the information and incorporated the Elemental and Æthyric aspects of the system into the degree work of the Order.

In Enochian magick, the elemental universe is represented by four large Elemental Tablets[5] (one each for Fire, Water, Air, and Earth) and a fifth tablet, (the Tablet of Union, or Spirit Tablet) which rules the other four in exactly the same way Spirit influences the four elements. These tablets are made up of squares upon which letters are inscribed. The letters make up the names of numerous angelic beings who can be called up or visited by the magician. I will discuss the details of the Elemental Tablets in the chapter on the Court Cards. For the moment let us turn our attention to the Spirit Tablet.

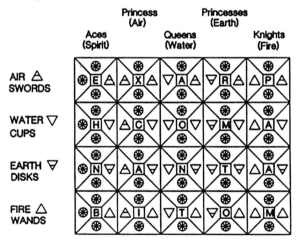

Figure 8. Enochian Tablet of Union (Spirit Tablet) showing placement of the four Aces and sixteen Court Cards of the Tarot.

---

5. See Appendix Three.

The Spirit Tablet is made up of twenty lettered squares which reveal the primary names of the four great spirits of the elements. EXARP is the spirit of Air, who rules the entire Elemental Tablet of Air; HCOMA is the spirit of Water, who rules the entire Elemental Tablet of Water; NANTA is the spirit of Earth, who rules the entire Elemental Tablet of Earth; and BITOM is the spirit of Fire, who rules the entire Elemental Tablet of Fire.

In keeping with the elemental formula, each square of the Spirit Tablet is divided into four sections. Because this is the Spirit Tablet, the top and bottom section of each square is attributed to Spirit ✹. The right section of each square is attributed to the element represented by each of the four horizontal *lines* of the tablet (△ – Air is found on the right section of each square of EXARP; ▽ – Water on the right section of each square of HCOMA; ▽ – Earth on the right section of each square of NANTA; and △ – Fire on the right section of each square of BITOM). The left section of each square is attributed to the element represented by each of the five vertical *columns* of the tablet.

As you can see, the EHNB column of the Spirit Tablet has the greatest ratio of Spirit sections. Each square is 3/4 Spirit and 1/4 the element of its row. Consequently E is the master ruler of both EXARP and the Elemental Tablet of Air; H the master ruler of HCOMA and the Elemental Tablet of Water; N is the master ruler of both NANTA and the Elemental Tablet of Earth; and B is the master ruler of both BITOM and the Elemental Tablet of Fire.

The four Aces of the Tarot serve the same purpose as the Spirit squares EHNB of the Enochian Spirit Tablet. In the *Tarot of Ceremonial Magick*, each of the four Aces displays both the applicable Enochian square from the Spirit Tablet (found in the lower left-hand corner), and lettered version of the entire Elemental Tablet it rules (found in the upper left-hand corner).

ENOCHIAN TEMPLE OPENINGS
AND CALLS — ELEMENTAL

To ceremonially access the various Enochian angelic beings represented by Aces, Court Cards, and Small Cards, the temple must be opened[6] in the appropriate element, and specific Calls, recited in the Angelic language, must be intoned. The text which accompanies the illustration of each card will indicate which openings and Calls are appropriate. These temple openings and Calls are found in Appendix Three of this book along with other pertinent information. The reader is advised to read all the material carefully and outline the sequence of actions before commencing operations.

ENOCHIAN CALLS —
THE THIRTY ÆTHYRS

There is a second great branch of Enochian magick that does not deal directly with elemental workings but rather concerns itself with the Enochian view of the heavens. Surrounding the elemental universe (represented by the four Elemental Tablets and the Tablet of Union) are thirty heavens or Æthyrs. The lowest Æthyr is TEX and is closest to the elemental universe, and the highest is LIL and represents the supreme attainment of the magician. The thirty Æthyrs roughly correspond in threes to the ten sephiroth of the Tree of Life, and are usually illustrated as thirty concentric circles surrounding the five tablets. A more accurate image would be of thirty transparent spheres, one inside another, like a glass onion.

---

6. The temple openings are identified by the traditional Rosicrucian grade system. These degrees represent a progressive climb up the Tree of Life and are given the following designations: 1°=10° for the element of Earth; 2°=9° for the element of Air; 3°=8° for the element of Water; and 4°=7° for the element of Fire. The first number thus represents the degree itself, and the second number represents the Sephira which that degree exemplifies.

These Æthyrs can theoretically be accessed simply by ceremonially intoning the nineteenth Enochian Call.[7] The magician, however, can fully access only as far as his or her level of illumination will permit. Starting with the 30th Æthyr and working up, almost everyone receives visions of the lower Æthyrs. The magician will eventually come to a point where he or she is denied a vision of the next Æthyr. By studying the records of his or her visions in previous sessions, the magician can get a very good idea of what obstacles remain in the way of spiritual advancement, and clues as to how to overcome these obstacles. Details of the Æthyric aspects of Enochian magick can be found in Appendix Three of this book.

THE TATTWA SYMBOLS

In addition to the Elemental Tablet and Spirit Tablet square, each Ace of the *Tarot of Ceremonial Magick* displays the Great Enochian Sigil of the element, found in the bottom center, and appropriate Hindu tattwa symbol, found on the lower right. The tattwa symbols have been used in the East for millennia as objects of concentration and meditation. Because of the purity of color and form of the tattwas, adepts of the Golden Dawn used them to astrally project into the various elements. The technique is very simple. The operator begins by gazing intently at the appropriate tattwa symbol for several minutes. He or she then turns their gaze to a blank, neutral colored background. A polarized image of the symbol remains momentarily floating before the operator who then imagines entering or projecting through the "ghost" image of the symbol. This is a disarmingly simple yet effective technique which allows the diligent practitioner to tap directly into the very source of occult knowledge. I can think of no better way to explore the true significance of the various cards.

The symbols are as follows: Spirit – Akasa – a black egg; Fire – Tejas – a red triangle (point up); Water – Apas – a sliver crescent; Air – Vayu – a blue circle; Earth – Prithvi – a yellow square.

---

7. The only variation between the Calls of the various Æthyrs is the name of the Æthyr itself found in the first sentence of the Nineteenth Call.

Aces are the Spirit representatives of their respective suits, so their tattwa symbols are composite; a black egg within a red triangle for the Ace of Wands; a black egg within a silver crescent for the Ace of Cups; a black egg within a blue circle for the Ace of Swords; and a black egg within a yellow square for the Ace of Disks. Composite tattwa symbols are also displayed upon each of the sixteen Court Cards.

ASTROLOGICAL ATTRIBUTIONS

The Aces are the primary representatives of their respective suits and elements; not the manifested elements themselves, but the spirit and seed of the elements. They are above and apart from the other Small Cards. They do not represent specific zodiac signs, degrees, or days of the year. Together with the four Princesses, the Aces rule quadrants of the heavens around the North Pole of the Earth. The meridian line intersects Giza and the elements rule in IHVH order going Eastward as follows: Wands covering Asia, Cups the area of the Pacific, Swords the Americas, and Disks Europe and Africa.

ACE OF WANDS

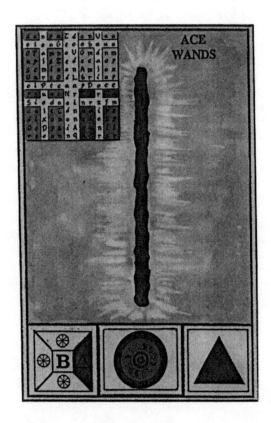

ROOT OF THE POWERS OF FIRE

Kether of Yetzirah

General divinatory meanings: Primordial energy as yet un-manifest. Seed of the will. Masculine archetype. Natural force. Beginnings.

Tattwa Symbol: Tejas-Akasa

Color: Brilliance

Enochian Attributions:

Tablet of Union: B of <u>B</u>ITOM

   Temple opening: Portal of the Vault of the Adepts

   Sequence of Calls: 1, 2 and 6

Elemental Tablet of Fire:

   Temple opening: Grade of $4° = 7°$

   Sequence of Calls: 6 only.

   Divine Names: oiP, **teaa, pDoce**

   King (Solar Senior): **edLprNaa**

   Seniors: "*...the gift of these Good Angels is to impart to mankind the knowledge and judgement of human affairs, etc.*"

Saturn: **arinnA**	Mars: **aaetPio**
Jupiter: **adoeoeT**	Mercury: **aNodoin**
Venus: **aapDoce**	Moon: **aLndUod**

(When invoking an individual Senior of the Fire Tablet, use the Hexagram Ritual appropriate to the planet following the temple opening in the grade of $4° = 7°$, and before recitation of the Sixth Call. When invoking angels of the subangles, the names of all six Seniors must be included in the conjuration.)

ACE OF CUPS

ROOT OF THE POWERS OF WATER

Kether of Briah

General divinatory meanings: Primordial receptivity. Seed of love. Feminine archetype.

Tattwa Symbol: Apas-Akasa

Color: White brilliance

Enochian Attributions:

Tablet of Union: H of <u>H</u>COMA

　　Temple opening: Portal of the Vault of the Adepts

　　Sequence of Calls: 1, 2 and 4

Elemental Tablet of Water:

　　Temple opening: Grade of $3°=8°$

　　Sequence of Calls: 4 only.

　　Divine Names: **mph, arsl, goiol**

　　King (Solar Senior): **raagiosl**

　　Seniors: "...*the gift of these Good Angels is to impart to mankind the knowledge and judgement of human affairs, etc.*"

Saturn: **ligdisa**	Mars: **lsrahpm**
Jupiter: **saiinou**	Mercury: **soniznt**
Venus: **slgaiol**	Moon: **laoaxrp**

(When invoking an individual Senior of the Water Tablet, use the Hexagram Ritual appropriate to the planet following the temple opening in the grade of $3°=8°$, and before recitation of the Fourth Call. When invoking angels of the subangles, the names of all six Seniors must be included in the conjuration.)

ACE OF SWORDS

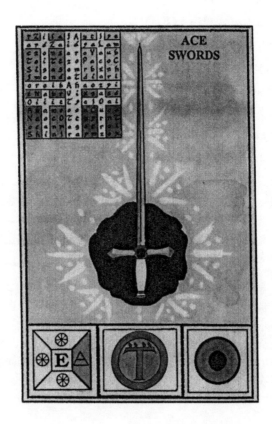

ROOT OF THE POWERS OF AIR

Kether of Yetzirah

General divinatory meanings: Primordial intelligence. Seed of the mind. Invoked force for good or ill.

Tattwa Symbol: Vayu-Akasa

Color: White brilliance

Enochian Attributions:

Tablet of Union: E of E̲XARP

   Temple opening: Portal of the Vault of the Adepts

   Sequence of Calls: 1, 2 and 3

Elemental Tablet of Air:

   Temple opening: Grade of 2°=9°

   Sequence of Calls: 3 only.

   Divine Names: **oro, ibAh, aozpi**

   King (Solar Senior): **baTaiVAh**

   Seniors: "*...the gift of these Good Angels is to impart to mankind the knowledge and judgement of human affairs, etc.*"

Saturn: **hipotga**	Mars: **hAbioro**
Jupiter: **Aaozaif**	Mercury: **AVToTar**
Venus: **Ahaozpi**	Moon: **hTmordA**

(When invoking an individual Senior of the Air Tablet, use the Hexagram Ritual appropriate to the planet following the temple opening in the grade of 2°=9°, and before recitation of the Third Call. When invoking angels of the subangles, the names of all six Seniors must be included in the conjuration.)

ACE OF DISKS

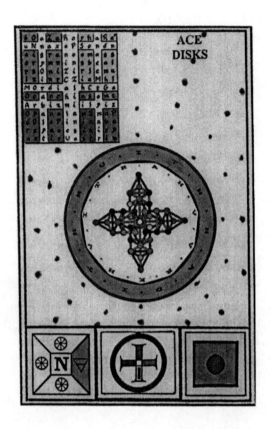

ROOT OF THE POWERS OF EARTH

Kether of Assiah

General divinatory meanings: Primordial matter. Seed of the material universe. Sun and Earth, spirit and flesh united.

Tattwa Symbol: Prithivi-Akasa

Color: White, flecked gold

Enochian Attributions:

Tablet of Union: N of <u>N</u>ANTA

Temple opening: Portal of the Vault of the Adepts

Sequence of Calls: 1, 2 and 5

Elemental Tablet of Earth:

Temple opening: Grade of 1°=10°

Sequence of Calls: 5 only.

Divine Names: **MOr, dial, hCtGa**

King (Solar Senior): **iCZhihal**

Seniors: "*…the gift of these Good Angels is to impart to mankind the knowledge and judgement of human affairs, etc.*"

Saturn: **liiansa**	Mars: **laidrOM**
Jupiter: **aCZinoR**	Mercury: **ahmlicU**
Venus: **alhCtGa**	Moon: **lZinoPo**

(When invoking an individual Senior of the Earth Tablet, use the Hexagram Ritual appropriate to the planet following the temple opening in the grade of 1°=10°, and before recitation of the Fifth Call. When invoking angels of the subangles, the names of all six Seniors must be included in the conjuration.)

CHAPTER FOUR

The Sixteen Court Cards

There are four Court Cards in each suit: Knight, Queen, Prince, and Princess. These are often used in tarot readings to represent actual people, but each of the Court Cards is also representative of a subdivision of one of the four elements.

The **Knights** represent the Fire aspect of their suits; the **Queens** represent the Water aspect of their suits, the **Princes** represent the Air aspect of their suits, and the **Princesses** represent the Earth aspect of their suits.

As I mentioned in an earlier chapter, the sixteen Court Cards have a direct parallel in the Enochian system of magick. They represent (and are represented by) the sixteen subangles (four per tablet) of the four Elemental Tablets.

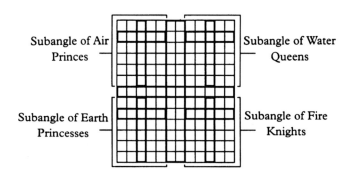

Figure 9. Positioning of the Court Cards upon the Enochian Elemental Tablets; positions identical in all four Tablets.

The positions of the four subangles are the same in all four Elemental Tablets; subangle of Air in the upper left; Water in the upper right; Earth in the lower left; and Fire in the lower right.

Each of the sixteen Court Cards of the *Tarot of Ceremonial Magick* displays the appropriate subangle at the bottom center of the card. The elemental sections of each of the squares are colored according to the following scale: Air – Yellow; Water – Blue, Earth – Green; and Fire – Red.

Each subangle contains thirty lettered squares which spell the names of a small hierarchy of angels. When invoking the angels of a subangle (Court Card), this hierarchy must be recognized and included in the wording of the conjuration. The appropriate temple opening ceremonies, Enochian Calls and conjurations are provided in their entirety in Appendix Three of this book.

I have reproduced below the Air subangle of the Fire Tablet (Prince of Wands) to illustrate how the names of the various angels of the subangles are determined. If you refer often to this diagram while reading what follows, you should have no trouble understanding the angelic hierarchy.

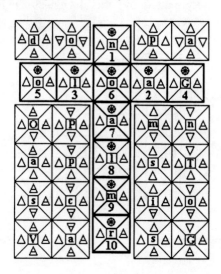

Figure 10. Air Subangle of the Elemental Tablet of Fire (Prince of Wands).

Each subangle is ruled by two divine names found on the calvary cross which divides it into sections; the first divine name is a six letter name found on the central vertical column read from top to bottom. In the case of subangle Air of Fire, **noalmr**. The second name is used to compel the angel **noalmr** to obedience. This is the five letter name of the horizontal arms of the calvary cross, **oloaG**.[1]

Next in hierarchical order is the Kerubic angel of the subangle. The four letter name of this angel is found above the arms of the cross, **dopa**.

The Kerubic angel rules the Four Lesser Angels found below the arms of the cross, **OPmn**, **apsT**, **scio**, and **VasG**.[2]

I now call the reader's attention to the individual squares of the subangle. Like all Enochian squares they are divided into four sections. There is a simple (almost) explanation of why the various squares are allotted elements which I will briefly review before we move on.

The Ten Squares of the Calvary Cross: The top section of each square of the calvary cross of every subangle is attributed to Spirit; the bottom section to a Sephira of the Tree of Life. The left section is always attributed to the element of the full tablet (in our example above, Fire), and the right section is attributed to the element represented by the subangle (in our example, Air).

The Four Squares of the Kerubic Angel: The top section of each of the four Kerubic squares is attributed to the element of the full tablet (in this case Fire), and the bottom section is attributed to the element represented by the subangle (in this case Air). You will notice that the left and right sections of a Kerubic square both represent the same element. In the case of our Air of Fire example: the right and left sections of the **d** square are both Air; the right and left sections of the **o** square are both Earth; the right and left sections of the **P** square are both Fire; and the right and left

---

1. Spelling and capitalization of the various names on the Elemental Tablets varies considerably throughout the original Dee material. The *Tarot of Ceremonial Magick* utilizes the lettering from the "reformed" tablets which represent perhaps the latest revisions of the tablets given by the spirits to Dee and Kelley.

2. See note at the end of this section.

sections of the a square are both Water. The order of the elements may change from subangle to subangle in conformity with a logical permutation. But what doesn't change is the fact that the order in which the elements appear in the squares of the Kerubic angel's name determines elemental characteristics of the four columns and four rows found below the arms of the cross. These sixteen squares contain the four-letter names of the Lesser Angels.

The Four Lesser Angels: Observe in Figure 10 (page 82) that the left section of each of the sixteen squares forming the names of the four lesser angels is always attributed to the element of the full Tablet, and the right section is always attributed to the element represented by the subangle. The elements of the top and bottom squares are determined by the pattern set by the order of the elements as they appear in the name of the Kerubic angel. In our example above, the order is (from left to right) Air, Earth, Fire, Water. Now view the sixteen squares of the lesser angels as four vertical columns:

O	P	m	n
a	p	s	T
s	c	i	o
V	a	s	G

Each of these columns is ruled by the Kerubic Square which is directly above it and the arm of the cross. The d square is the Air square. Consequently all the top sections of **OasV** are attributed to Air; **Ppca** to Earth; **msis** to Fire; and **nToG** to Water.

Now view the sixteen squares of the lesser angels as four horizontal rows. The bottom sections of each of these squares is similarly governed by the order of the Kerubic squares. Starting with the bottom name **Vasg**, the bottom sections are attributed to Air; **scio** to Earth; **apsT** to Fire; and **OPmn** to Water.

O	P	m	n
a	p	s	T
s	c	i	o
V	a	s	G

The angelic Calls necessary to activate the various tablets and call forth the Enochian spirits can be found in Appendix Three of this book along with the appropriate ceremonial temple openings.

The above description may seem hopelessly confusing, especially to the novice. But I assure you it is much easier than it sounds. A good way to see how simple it really is, is to color the tablets found in Appendix Three. By doing so you will readily see the logic of the system and also be rewarded with a beautiful set of tablets.

Within the structure of Enochian magick additional angel names can be determined by changing the order of the four letters making up the name of the Kerubic angel. These additional Kerubs in turn rule four lesser angels (below the arms of the cross) whose names are formed by rearranging the letters in the same order as those of the rearranged Kerub.

Also, by prefixing the names of the Kerubic and lesser angels with appropriate letters from the Tablet of Union, the names of additional ruling angels can be determined. These angels could be thought of as archangelic in nature and positioned in conjurations after the divine names of the calvary cross in the Enochian hierarchy. The rules governing these and other variations are complex, and considerable disagreement exists, even among the most knowledgeable experts on the matter, concerning exactly which letters from the Tablet of Union are the appropriate prefixes.

Conversely, each subangle contains the triliteral names of four malevolent spirits or cacodaemones or who by tradition manifest the averse characteristics of their angelic neighbors [i.e., the sixteen Lesser Angels of the four subangles of Air (the four Prince Court Cards of the Tarot) are "skilled and effective in Medicine and the cure of sickness" but the cacodaemones of those same subangles bring sickness and disease]. Their names are formed by joining the two letters on the left side of the vertical column of the calvary cross with a specific letter from the Tablet of Union. Unlike the other aspects of Enochian magick, information concerning the appropriate uses for these spirits and details outlining safe techniques whereby they can be conjured and controled are conspicuously absent (or buried very deeply) in traditional Enochian literature. For the sake of completeness, I have listed their names with the other relevant information about the Court Cards, but I do not suggest a program of magical experimentation with the cacodaemones without a great deal of preliminary research and a mature and profound understanding of the possible consequences. If you are truly interested in mastering the many aspects of Enochian magick, I encourage you to avail yourself of the many fine texts on the subject which are currently available, especially *Elizabethan Magic*[3] by Robert Turner (see Bibliography).

ASTROLOGICAL ATTRIBUTIONS OF THE COURT CARDS

The four Knights, Queens, and Princes[4] each rule thirty degrees of the Zodiac—from 20° of one sign to 20° of the next. There are good reasons for this zodiacal mix of elemental signs in the character of the Court Cards. First of all the twelve signs of the zodiac are already represented in the tarot by twelve Trumps: Emperor, Hierophant, Lovers, Chariot, Lust, Hermit, Justice, Death, Art, Devil, Star, and Moon. Secondly, it is the nature of the elements to combine with other elements. Elemental creation is by nature a churning process. By including ten degrees of the previous sign in their composition, the Knights, Queens, and Princes more accurately reflect the elemental facts of nature. In keeping with the concept of churning, it is the Queen of each suit, not the Knight, which represents the cardinal aspect of the element's nature. This is why we find the Queens to be the predominant rulers of the cardinal signs of the zodiac.

This information and the approximate days of the year covered by these thirty-degree periods is displayed in the upper right section of each of the Court Cards of the *Tarot of Ceremonial Magick*. Using this information, the Significator in a tarot reading can be determined by the questioner's birthday, and other individuals relevant to the reading can be similarly identified.[5]

---

3. (Shaftesbury, England: Element Books, 1989).
4. The four Princesses do not represent degrees of the zodiac. As mentioned earlier, they rule with the Aces the four quadrants of heaven about the North Pole of the Earth.
5. See Appendix One of this book for a complete graph.

I CHING HEXAGRAMS

The *I Ching* (Chinese *Book of Changes*) has been called the Qabalah of the East. The *Tarot of Ceremonial Magick* does not presume to act as a replacement to this venerable work and divinatory tool, but there are certain areas where the Qabalah and *I Ching* clearly coincide.

There are sixty-four hexagrams in the *I Ching*. (A hexagram is a figure made up of six lines, either broken [Yin – female] or unbroken [Yang – male]). Each Hexagram is made up of two trigrams (figures made up of three lines, either broken or unbroken). There are eight such trigrams representing Male, Female, Sun, Moon, Fire, Water, Air, and Earth. Of these, the four elemental trigrams perfectly parallel the four elements of the tarot.

Fire	Water	Air	Earth

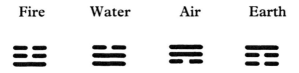

*Figure 11. The Four Elemental Trigrams
of the* I Ching.

When combined to form hexagrams (Fire of Fire, Water of Fire, Earth of Air, etc.) the resulting sixteen figures perfectly match the elemental characteristics of the sixteen Court Cards. These hexagrams can be found on the upper left of each of the Court Cards and their titles and brief divinatory meanings can be found in the text following the illustration of each Court Card. As it is sometimes difficult to interpret the meanings of the Court Cards in a tarot reading it can be very helpful to consult the corresponding *I Ching* hexagram for greater insight. For a more in-depth understanding of the *I Ching*, I encourage you to obtain one of the many fine translations of the text currently available, and refer to it often in conjunction with your use of the *Tarot of Ceremonial Magick*.

KNIGHT OF WANDS

Lord of the Flame and the Lightning; King of the Spirits of Fire

FIRE OF FIRE

20° Scorpio to 20° Sagittarius (November 13 to December 12)

General divinatory meanings: A proud, generous man. Sometimes impulsive or brutal. *Action, but indicates failure if not successful on first try.*

I Ching Hexagram: #51. The Arousing (Shock, Thunder). *Development. Moving power. Relief and merriment following a shocking experience.*

Tattwa Symbol: Tejas-Tejas

Enochian Attributions:

Tablet of Union: **M** of **BITO<u>M</u>**

    Temple opening #1: Portal of the Vault of the Adepts

    Sequence of Calls: 1 and 2

    Temple opening #2: Grade of $4° = 7°$

    Sequence of Calls: 6 only

Elemental Tablet: Fire Subangle of Fire Tablet

    Temple opening: Grade of $4° = 7°$

    Sequence of Calls: 6 only

Angels of the Subangle:

    Divine Names: **rzionr** calls forth the powers of the Subangle. **nrzfm** compels **rzionr** to obedience.

    Kerub: **ZiZA**

Good Angels: ...that comprehend the species and uses of the living creatures in the Element of Fire.

adre

sisp

pali

ACar

Cacodaemones: **Rad, Asi, Xpa,** and **Eac.**

QUEEN OF WANDS
Queen of the Throne of Flame

WATER OF FIRE

20° Pisces to 20° Aries (March 11 to April 10)

General divinatory meanings: A generous, attractive woman with a great capacity for love, but on her own terms. Sometimes fickle, obstinate and melancholic. *Constructive work under the guidance of another.*

I Ching Hexagram: #17. Following. *Supreme success. Be considerate. If you would rule, first learn to serve.*

Tattwa Symbol: Tejas-Apas

Enochian Attributions:

Tablet of Union: T of BI<u>T</u>OM

>*Temple opening #1:* Portal of the Vault of the Adepts

>*Sequence of Calls:* 1 and 2

>*Temple opening #2:* Grade of 4°=7°

>*Sequence of Calls:* 6 only

Elemental Tablet: Water Subangle of Fire Tablet

>*Temple opening:* Grade of 4°=7°

>*Sequence of Calls:* 6 and 17

Angels of the Subangle:

>*Divine Names:* **Vadali** calls forth the powers of the Subangle. **obaua** compels **Vadali** to obedience.

>*Kerub:* **anaa**

Good Angels: ...skilled and potent in the discovery, collecting, use and intrinsic power of metals, and also in the combining of stones and their powers.

Gmnm
ecop
Amox
brap

Cacodaemones: **Mgm, Oec, Cam,** and **Hbr.**

PRINCE OF WANDS

Prince of the Chariot of Fire

AIR OF FIRE

20° Cancer to 20° Leo (July 12 to August 11)

General divinatory meanings: An impetuous young man, strong and energetic. A practical joker. Can be a cowardly braggart, sadistic and callous. *Struggling against the odds, but winning the very long run.*

I Ching Hexagram: #42. Increase. *Undertakings indicated if immediate action can be taken. Imitate that which you admire.*

Tattwa Symbol: Tejas-Vayu

Enochian Attributions:

Tablet of Union: I of B̲ITOM

    Temple opening #1: Portal of the Vault of the Adepts

    Sequence of Calls: 1 and 2

    Temple opening #2: Grade of $4°=7°$

    Sequence of Calls: 6 only

Elemental Tablet: Air Subangle of Fire Tablet

    Temple opening: Grade of $4°=7°$

    Sequence of Calls: 6 and 16

Angels of the Subangle:

    Divine Names: **noalmr** calls forth the powers of the Subangle. **oloaG** compels **noalmr** to obedience.

    Kerub: **dopa**

Good Angels: ...*most skilled and effective in Medicine and the cure of sickness.*

                OPmn
                apmn
                scio
                VasG

Cacodaemones: **Mop, Oap, Csc,** and **Hva.**

PRINCESS OF WANDS

Princess of the Shining Flame; Rose of the Palace of Fire

EARTH OF FIRE

With the Ace of Wands rules ♋ ♌ ♍ Quadrant
above North Pole and Asia.

General divinatory meanings: A reckless, extremely individualistic young woman, ambitious and self-centered. Sometimes domineering, vindictive and irrational. *"Know that when you play with me, you play with fire."*

I Ching Hexagram: #27. Nourishment. *Be careful with your words. Observe the source of ones' nourishment.*

Tattwa Symbol: Tejas-Prithivi

Enochian Attributions:

Tablet of Union: O of BIT<u>O</u>M

>*Temple opening #1:* Portal of the Vault of the Adepts

>*Sequence of Calls:* 1 and 2

>*Temple opening #2:* Grade of 4°=7°

>*Sequence of Calls:* 6 only

Elemental Tablet: Earth Subangle of Fire Tablet

>*Temple opening:* Grade of 4°=7°

>*Sequence of Calls:* 6 and 18

Angels of the Subangle:

>*Divine Names:* **uolxDo** calls forth the powers of the Subangle. **Sioda** compels **uolxDo** to obedience.

>*Kerub:* **psac**

>*Good Angels:* ...*most skilled and powerful in Transformations.*
>>**datT**
>>**diom**
>>**Oopz**
>>**rgan**

Cacodaemones: **Rda, Adi, Xoo,** and **Erg.**

KNIGHT OF CUPS

Lord of the Waves and the Waters; King of the Hosts of the Sea

FIRE OF WATER

20° Aquarius to 20° Pisces (February 9 to March 10)

General divinatory meanings: An amiable man of innocence and purity, a dilettante. May be passive-aggressive in temperament, and tormented by conflicting elements of his nature. *Failure, unless extraordinary good fortune intervenes.*

I Ching Hexagram: #54. The Marrrying Maiden. *Nothing furthers. Tactful reserve is indicated.*

Tattwa Symbol: Apas-Tejas

Enochian Attributions:

Tablet of Union: A of HCOM<u>A</u>

>*Temple opening #1:* Portal of the Vault of the Adepts

>*Sequence of Calls:* 1 and 2

>*Temple opening #2:* Grade of $3° = 8°$

>*Sequence of Calls:* 4 only

Elemental Tablet: Fire Subangle of Water Tablet

>*Temple opening:* Grade of $3° = 8°$

>*Sequence of Calls:* 4 and 12

Angels of the Subangle:

>*Divine Names:* **iaaasd** calls forth the powers of the Subangle. **aTapa** compels **iaaasd** to obedience.

>*Kerub:* **nLrx**

Good Angels: ...that comprehend the species and uses of the living creatures in the Element of Water.

xPcn

Vasa

dApi

rni

Cacodaemones: **Rxp, Ava, Xda,** and **Ern.**

QUEEN OF CUPS

Queen of the Thrones of Water

WATER OF WATER

20° Gemini to 20° Cancer (June 11 to July 11)

General divinatory meanings: An inscrutable woman, attractive and popular; completely reflective of every impression she receives. *Beware of flattery; others see only themselves in you.*

I Ching Hexagram: #58. The Joyous, Lake. *Pleasure. Gentleness brings cheerful support from friends.*

Tattwa Symbol: Apas-Apas

Enochian Attributions:

Tablet of Union: O of HC**O**MA

Temple opening #1: Portal of the Vault of the Adepts

Sequence of Calls: 1 and 2

Temple opening #2: Grade of 3°=8°

Sequence of Calls: 4 only

Elemental Tablet: Water Subangle of Water Tablet

Temple opening: Grade of 3°=8°

Sequence of Calls: 4 only

Angels of the Subangle:

Divine Names: **nelaPr** calls forth the powers of the Subangle. **omebb** compels **nelaPr** to obedience.

Kerub: **tDim**

Good Angels: ...skilled and potent in the discovery, collecting, use and intrinsic power of metals, and also in the combining of stones and their powers.

maGm
leoc
Vss
rVoi

Cacodaemones: **Mma, Ole, Cvs,** and **Hru.**

PRINCE OF CUPS

Prince of the Chariot of the Waters

AIR OF WATER

20° Libra to 20° Scorpio (October 13 to November 12)

General divinatory meanings: A mysterious subtle, intensely passionate man, without conscience as ordinarily understood. Can be the victim of his own over-reaching ambition. *The essentials of success are goodwill, sincerity and right mating.*

I Ching Hexagram: #61. Inner Truth. *Sincerity. Good fortune. Rid yourself of prejudice and become empathetic before passing judgment.*

Tattwa Symbol: Apas-Vayu

Enochian Attributions:

Tablet of Union: C of H<u>C</u>OMA

> *Temple opening #1:* Portal of the Vault of the Adepts
>
> *Sequence of Calls:* 1 and 2
>
> *Temple opening #2:* Grade of 3°=8°
>
> *Sequence of Calls:* 4 only

Elemental Tablet: Air Subangle of Water Tablet

> *Temple opening:* Grade of 3°=8°
>
> *Sequence of Calls:* 4 and 10

Angels of the Subangle:

> *Divine Names:* **Obgota** calls forth the powers of the Subangle. **aabco** compels **Obgota** to obedience.
>
> *Kerub:* tAaD

Good Angels: ...most skilled and effective in Medicine and the cure of sickness.

Toco

nhdD

paAx

Saix

Cacodaemones: **Mto, Onh, Cpa,** and **Hsa.**

PRINCESS OF CUPS

Princess of the Waters;
Lotus of the Palace of the Floods

EARTH OF WATER

With the Ace of Cups rules ♎ ♏ ♐ Quadrant
above North Pole, and the Pacific.

General divinatory meanings: An extraordinarily gracious young woman who effortlessly radiates all sweetness voluptuousness and romance. *A symbiotic relationship.*

I Ching Hexagram: #41. Decrease. *In times of diminishing resources simplicity prevails.*

Tattwa Symbol: Apas-Prithivi

Enochian Attributions:

Tablet of Union: M of HCO<u>M</u>A

>*Temple opening #1:* Portal of the Vault of the Adepts

>*Sequence of Calls:* 1 and 2

>*Temple opening #2:* Grade of $3°=8°$

>*Sequence of Calls:* 4 only

Elemental Tablet: Earth Subangle of Water Tablet

>*Temple opening:* Grade of $3°=8°$

>*Sequence of Calls:* 4 and 11

Angels of the Subangle:

>*Divine Names:* **maLadi** calls forth the powers of the Subangle. **olaaD** compels **maLadi** to obedience.

>*Kerub:* **Magl**

Good Angels: ...*most skilled and powerful in Transformations.*

paco
ndzN
iiPo
xrnh

Cacodaemones: **Rpa, And, Xii,** and **Exr.**

KNIGHT OF SWORDS

Lord of the Winds and Breezes;
King of the Spirits of Air

FIRE OF AIR

20° Taurus to 20° Gemini (May 11 to June 10)

General divinatory meanings: A delicate man, yet active, fierce and courageous; often the victim of his own shortsightedness or ill-conceived notions. *Attack.*

I Ching Hexagram: #32. Duration. *Do not change direction. Continue forward.*

Tattwa Symbol: Vayu-Tejas

Enochian Attributions:

Tablet of Union: P of **EXAR<u>P</u>**

Temple opening #1: Portal of the Vault of the Adepts

Sequence of Calls: 1 and 2

Temple opening #2: Grade of $2° = 9°$

Sequence of Calls: 3 only

Elemental Tablet: Fire Subangle of Air Tablet

Temple opening: Grade of $2° = 9°$

Sequence of Calls: 3 and 9

Angels of the Subangle:

Divine Names: **aOurrz** calls forth the powers of the Subangle. **alOai** compels **aOurrz** to obedience.

Kerub: **xgsd**

Good Angels: *...that comprehend the species and uses of the living creatures in the Element of Air.*

acca
npnT
otoi
pmox

Cacodaemones: **Cac, Onp, Mot,** and **Apm.**

QUEEN OF SWORDS
Queen of the Thrones of Air

WATER OF AIR

20° Virgo to 20° Libra (September 12 to October 12)

General divinatory meanings: An aggressive woman, keenly perceptive. In action, confident; in spirit, gracious and just. Graceful, perhaps a dancer. Sometimes cruel, deceitful, and unreliable. *Support comes from seemingly unsuitable sources.*

I Ching Hexagram: #28. Preponderance of the Great. *Critical mass has been reached. Seek an avenue of transition. Quick action is indicated if danger is to be avoided.*

Tattwa Symbol: Vayu-Apas

Enochian Attributions:

Tablet of Union: A of EX**A**RP

> *Temple opening #1:* Portal of the Vault of the Adepts
>
> *Sequence of Calls:* 1 and 2
>
> *Temple opening #2:* Grade of $2°=9°$
>
> *Sequence of Calls:* 3 only

Elemental Tablet: Water Subangle of Air Tablet

> *Temple opening:* Grade of $2°=9°$
>
> *Sequence of Calls:* 3 and 7

Angels of the Subangle:

> *Divine Names:* lLacza calls forth the powers of the Subangle. **paLam** compels **iLacza** to obedience.
>
> *Kerub:* **ytpa**

Good Angels: ...skilled and potent in the discovery, collecting, use and intrinsic power of metals, and also in the combining of stones and their powers.

oYvb
PaoC
rbnh
diri

Cacodaemones: **Xoy, Apa, Rrb,** and **Pdi.**

PRINCE OF SWORDS
Prince of the Chariot of the Winds

AIR OF AIR
20° Capricorn to 20° Aquarius (January 10 to February 8)

General divinatory meanings: An ambivalent young man, bright yet unfocused. A fanatic, easily attracted to fads, cults, causes and drugs. Can be overcautious, indecisive and unreliable. *Success possible, but only through the aid of an intelligence greater than your own.*

I Ching Hexagram: #57. The Penetrating, Wind. *Flexibility. Vacillation. Time is on your side. Success in small matters.*

Tattwa Symbol: Vayu-Vayu

Enochian Attributions:

Tablet of Union: X of E<u>X</u>ARP

> *Temple opening #1:* Portal of the Vault of the Adepts
>
> *Sequence of Calls:* 1 and 2
>
> *Temple opening #2:* Grade of $2°=9°$
>
> *Sequence of Calls:* 3 only

Elemental Tablet: Air Subangle of Air Tablet

> *Temple opening:* Grade of $2°=9°$
>
> *Sequence of Calls:* 3 only

Angels of the Subangle:

> *Divine Names:* **idoigo** calls forth the powers of the Subangle. **ardZa** compels idoigo to obedience.
>
> *Kerub:* **rZla**

Good Angels: ...most skilled and effective in Medicine and the cure of sickness.

czns
ToTt
Sias
fmnd

Cacodaemones: **Xcz, Ato, Rsi,** and **Pfm.**

PRINCESS OF SWORDS

Princess of the Rushing Winds;
Lotus of the Palace of Air

EARTH OF AIR

With the Ace of Swords rules ♑ ♒ ♓ Quadrant
above North Pole, and the Americas.

General divinatory meanings: An aggressive woman with great
cleverness in the management of practical affairs and the settlement
of controversies. Can be anxiety ridden, and crushed by responsibilities, especially those of family. *Sometimes it is all right to abandon
responsibilities.*

I Ching Hexagram: #18. Decay. *Troublesome services. Hard work. What you have ruined you can repair.*

Tattwa Symbol: Vayu-Prihivi

Enochian Attributions:

Tablet of Union: R of **EXARP**

    Temple opening #1: Portal of the Vault of the Adepts

    Sequence of Calls: 1 and 2

    Temple opening #2: Grade of 2°=9°

    Sequence of Calls: 3 only

Elemental Tablet: Earth Subangle of Air Tablet

    Temple opening: Grade of 2°=9°

    Sequence of Calls: 3 and 8

Angels of the Subangle:

    Divine Names: **aiaoai** calls forth the powers of the Subangle. **Oiit** compels **aiaoai** to obedience.

    Kerub: **tNbr**

Good Angels: ...*most skilled and powerful in Transformations.*
           Abmo
           NacO
           ocnm
           Shal

Cacodaemones: **Cab, Ona, Moc,** and **Ash.**

KNIGHT OF DISKS

Lord of the Wide and Fertile Land; King of the Spirits of Earth

FIRE OF EARTH

20° Leo to 20° Virgo (August 12 to September 11)

General divinatory meanings: A sturdy man with good instincts, a breadwinner, perhaps a farmer. Unintellectual, laborious, proccupied with material things. Can be shortsighted, stupid and superstitious. *Use your instincts. Success results from imitating nature.*

I Ching Hexagram: #62. Preponderance of the Small. *Success in trifles. Success at this time is not indicated for great matters.*

Tattwa Symbol: Prithivi-Tejas

Enochian Attributions:

Tablet of Union: A of NANT<u>A</u>

Temple opening #1: Portal of the Vault of the Adepts

Sequence of Calls: 1 and 2

Temple opening #2: Grade of $1° = 10°$

Sequence of Calls: 5 only

Elemental Tablet: Fire Subangle of Earth Tablet

Temple opening: Grade of $1° = 10°$

Sequence of Calls: 5 and 15

Angels of the Subangle:

Divine Names: **opmnir** calls forth the powers of the Subangle. **ilpiz** compels **opmnir** to obedience.

Kerub: **asmt**

Good Angels: ...that comprehend the species and uses of the living creatures in the Element of Earth.

mSaP

iaba

izxp

stim

Cacodaemones: **Cms, Oia, Miz,** and **Ast.**

QUEEN OF DISKS

Queen of the Thrones of Earth

WATER OF EARTH

20° Sagittarius to 20° Capricorn (December 13 to January 9)

General divinatory meanings: A quite, practical woman, affectionate, domesticated and kind. Often shyly lustful. May attempt to seek relief from drudgery by alcohol or drugs. *Quietly move forward. No need to battle circumstances.*

I Ching Hexagram: #31. Wooing. *Courtship, not seduction, is indicated. Taking a wife brings good fortune.*

Tattwa Symbol: Prithivi-Apas

Enochian Attributions:

Tablet of Union: N of NA<u>N</u>TA

 Temple opening #1: Portal of the Vault of the Adepts

 Sequence of Calls: 1 and 2

 Temple opening #2: Grade of 1°=10°

 Sequence of Calls: 5 only

Elemental Tablet: Water Subangle of Earth Tablet

 Temple opening: Grade of 1°=10°

 Sequence of Calls: 5 and 14

Angels of the Subangle:

 Divine Names: **anaeeM** calls forth the powers of the Subangle. **Sondn** compels **anaeeM** to obedience.

 Kerub: **phRa**

Good Angels: *...skilled and potent in the discovery, collecting, use and intrinsic power of metals, and also in the combining of stones and their powers.*

omgg
gbal
rlmv
iahl

Cacodaemones: **Xom, Agb, Rrl,** and **Pia.**

PRINCE OF DISKS
Prince of the Chariot of Earth

AIR OF EARTH

20° Aries to 20° Taurus (April 11 to May 10)

General divinatory meanings: An energetic and competent man, steadfast, trustworthy, ingenious; both the jack *and* the master of all trades. Almost emotionless, he may appear insensitive. *Gradual liberation from repressive conditions.*

I Ching Hexagram: #53. Gradual Progress. *A fortunate marriage. Observe all formalities. Compusive action would be unwise.*

Tattwa Symbol: Prithivi-Vayu

Enochian Attributions:

Tablet of Union: A of N<u>A</u>NTA

    Temple opening #1: Portal of the Vault of the Adepts

    Sequence of Calls: 1 and 2

    Temple opening #2: Grade of $1°=10°$

    Sequence of Calls: 5 only

Elemental Tablet: Air Subangle of Earth Tablet

    Temple opening: Grade of $1°=10°$

    Sequence of Calls: 5 and 13

Angels of the Subangle:

    Divine Names: **angpOi** calls forth the powers of the Subangle. **uNnax** compels **angpOi** to obedience.

    Kerub: **bOZa**

Good Angels: ...most skilled and effective in Medicine and the cure of sickness.

aira

ormn

rsni

iznr

Cacodaemones: **Xai, Aor, Rrs,** and **Piz.**

PRINCESS OF DISKS

Princess of the Echoing Hills;
Rose of the Palace of Earth

EARTH OF EARTH

With the Ace of Disks rules ♈ ♉ ♊ Quadrant
above North Pole, and Europe and Africa.

General divinatory meanings: A strong and beautiful woman,
perhaps a mother. Ideal projection of womanhood. So all-encom-
passing in her attributes she may appear confusingly inconsistent.
She rests and awaits the future. *The threshold of transformation.*

I Ching Hexagram: #52. Peace. Mountain. *Withdraw inward and achieve a quiet heart.*

Tattwa Symbol: Prithivi-Prithivi

Enochian Attributions:

Tablet of Union: T of NAN**T**A

    Temple opening #1: Portal of the Vault of the Adepts

    Sequence of Calls: 1 and 2

    Temple opening #2: Grade of $1° = 10°$

    Sequence of Calls: 5 only

Elemental Tablet: Earth Subangle of Earth Tablet

    Temple opening: Grade of $1° = 10°$

    Sequence of Calls: 5 only

Angels of the Subangle:

    Divine Names: **abalpt** calls forth the powers of the Subangle. **Arbiz** compels **abalpt** to obedience.

    Kerub: **Ocnc**

    Good Angels: ...*most skilled and powerful in Transformations.*
                    Opna
                    dOoP
                    rxao
                    axir

Cacodaemones: **Cop, Odo, Mrx,** and **Aax.**

CHAPTER FIVE

The Thirty-Six Small Cards

Now we move to the very rim of the great wheel of the tarot. The remaining thirty-six cards are the Twos through Tens of the four suits. These cards, with titles like LOVE, SORROW, ABUNDANCE, DEFEAT, WEALTH, are often the most helpful in tarot readings because they appear to deal directly with the mundane matters of love, health, business and the immediate future. While not ignoring the efficacy of the Small Cards as divinatory tools, the *Tarot of Ceremonial Magick* also uncovers a treasure-house of hidden information that can be of invaluable aid to the student and practitioner of magick. But before we dig for those treasures we should answer some very fundamental questions:

Why are the Small Cards titled the way they are? Why is the Two of Cups called LOVE and the Three of Swords called SORROW? Or why is the Five of Wands STRIFE but the Six of Wands VICTORY? Were these titles and attributes arbitrarily created? Are they purely traditional? There is an answer.

The titles and meanings of the thirty-six Small Cards are determined by three hermetic variables. The first two are astrological and the third purely qabalistic.

Hang on. Its easier than you think!

Variable # 1. Zodiacal attribution.

Each of the thirty-six Small Cards represents ten degrees (one decan) of the zodiac. In groups of threes, the nine Wands represent the fire signs (Aries, Leo, Sagittarius), the nine Cups represent the water signs (Cancer, Scorpio, Pisces), the nine Swords represent

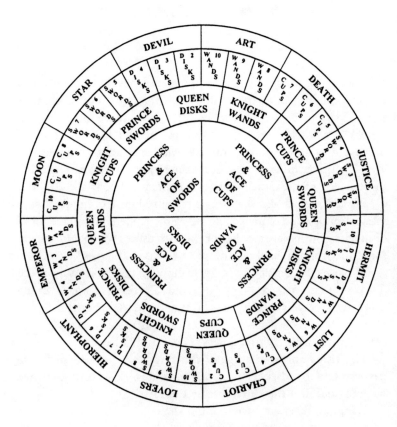

*Figure 12. The great astrological wheel of the tarot;
the completed qabalistic mandala.*

the air signs (Libra, Aquarius, Gemini), the nine Disks represent the earth signs (Capricorn, Taurus, Virgo).

Twos, Threes, and Fours represent the Cardinal Signs: Aries – Fire, Cancer – Water, Libra – Air, Capricorn – Earth.

Fives, Sixes, and Sevens represent the Fixed Signs: Leo – Fire, Scorpio – Water, Aquarius – Air, Taurus – Earth.

Eights, Nines, and Tens represent the Mutable Signs: Sagittarius – Fire, Pisces – Water, Gemini – Air, Virgo – Earth.

The exact degrees and the approximate days of the year that these cards represent are displayed in the upper right section of each of the Small Cards of the *Tarot of Ceremonial Magick.* Starting at 0° Aries and placed in the following order, the entire year is chronologically represented in perfect order:

2 – 3 – 4 of	Wands —	Aries	Cardinal	Fire
5 – 6 – 7 of	Disks —	Taurus	Fixed	Earth
8 – 9 – 10 of	Swords —	Gemini	Mutable	Air
2 – 3 – 4 of	Cups —	Cancer	Cardinal	Water
5 – 6 – 7 of	Wands —	Leo	Fixed	Fire
8 – 9 – 10 of	Disks —	Virgo	Mutable	Earth
2 – 3 – 4 of	Swords —	Libra	Cardinal	Air
5 – 6 – 7 of	Cups —	Scorpio	Fixed	Water
8 – 9 – 10 of	Wands —	Sagittarius	Mutable	Fire
2 – 3 – 4 of	Disks —	Capricorn	Cardinal	Earth
5 – 6 – 7 of	Swords —	Aquarius	Fixed	Air
8 – 9 – 10 of	Cups —	Pisces	Mutable	Water

The reader is encouraged to lay out a great counter-clockwise circle using the Small Cards arranged in the above order. Then place the Knights, Queens, and Princes next to the three Small Cards which together represent the same degrees and days of the year. In this way it is easy to see how the Court Cards rule the various Small Cards. Now place the Princesses and their respective Aces together in a cross or square in the center of your circle. Looking down at this figure it is as though you are looking down upon the North Pole of the Earth, and the great circle of cards girdling the equator represents the belt of the zodiac (figure 12).

Variable # 2. Planetary attribution.

In addition to a zodiacal attribution, a planet has been allocated to each of the thirty-six Small Cards. Beginning with the 5 of Wands (0° Leo, the traditional Chaldean start of the year), and moving by decans through the year, the planets are assigned in the following qabalistic order: Saturn, Jupiter, Mars, Sun, Venus, Mercury, Moon.[1] This pattern is repeated until all thirty-six decans have been assigned a planet.[2]

The planetary/zodiacal information is displayed in two areas of each of the Small Cards of the *Tarot of Ceremonial Magick*; underneath the title at bottom center, and upon the Enochian square taken from the Grand Cross portion of the Elemental Tablets. This square is displayed in the upper left of each Small Card.

Now we have named the first two variables in determining the title and characteristic of a Small Card. With this information alone we can already tell a great deal about it. The Two of Wands, DOMINION, for example, has the astrological attribution of Mars in the very compatible Sign of Aries (Mars rules Aries). The qualities of Dominion are expressed nicely by Mars in Aries, but there is one more variable to be considered before the true characteristic of a Small Card can be determined—the number and suit of the card.

---

1. Sephiroth 3 through 9 on the Tree of Life have the following planetary attributions: 3–Saturn, 4–Jupiter, 5–Mars, 6–Sun, 7–Venus, 8–Mercury, and 9–Moon. This order is followed in allocating planets to the thirty-six Small Cards.

2. As there are seven planets and thirty-six decans, the ancient astrologers were faced with one left-over decan. This they corrected (you knew they would) by repeating an assignment of Mars to both the last decan of winter (20°–30° Pisces, 10 of Cups), and the first decan of spring (0°–10° Aries, 2 of Wands. In this way they acknowledged an extra dose of the fiery energy of Mars which is needed to overcome winter's inertia and help usher in the spring.

Variable #3. Position on the Tree of Life.

We recall that there are four qabalistic worlds, each representing a letter in the divine Name IHVH. Each of these worlds is represented by a tarot suit, and each world contains its own Tree of Life. Each Sephira of the four descending worlds has its own traditional correspondences and attributes. These characteristics along with the astrological attributes of each Small Card are weighed to determine the overall nature and title of each Small Card.

Examples: **Five of Wands, STRIFE.** Saturn (planet of restriction) in Leo (sign of power and fiery energy) the 5th Sephira (Geburah, Sephira sometimes called Pachad—Terror) = Strife.

Six of Wands, VICTORY. Jupiter (beneficent planet of fortune, expansion, and order) in Leo (sign of power and fiery energy) in the 6th Sephira (Tiphareth, Sephira of beauty, and supreme balance) = Victory.

Five of Disks, MATERIAL TROUBLE. Mercury (planet of swift, intellectual energy) in Taurus (the heavy, slow, fixed sign of earth; the very opposite type of energy of Mercury) in the 5th Sephira (Geburah, see above) = Material Trouble.

Each of the Small Cards can thus be worked out by considering the three variables as we have done above.

THE ANGELS OF THE SHEMHAMPHORASH

The seventy-two angels of the Shemhamphorash (divided name of God) are the traditional qabalistic rulers of the thirty-six Small Cards. Assigned in pairs to each Small Card, they each represent five degrees of their host decan. These angels can be called upon to bestow greater insight upon the inner meanings of each card, or can be evoked to manifest the energy represented by the cards. Their names are found just above the Goetic seals on the lower right and left of the cards. The angel on the left rules the first five degrees of the decan, the one on the right the next five degrees. How these names were obtained is an interesting story, and very illustrative of qabalistic logic.

It seems that sometime in the distant yet undetermined past, a student of the qabalah had undertaken the task of counting the letters in each verse of the Hebrew scriptures and recording his findings. (I can only assume this task was some form of monastic punishment.) Nevertheless it was discovered that verses 19, 20, and 21 of the 14th chapter of *Exodus*[3] each contained seventy-two Hebrew letters. Assuming this phenomenon to be a divine revelation, the qabalists wrote the verses out in three lines in the following manner: Verse 19 was written normally (right to left). Directly beneath this they did the same with verse 20, only this verse they wrote out from left to right. Finally verse 21 was placed beneath verse 20 written from right to left. When read in vertical columns they discovered seventy-two three-letter words. It was decided that this whole assembly was the seventy-two fold name of God. To exercise the Divine Will each of these seventy-two aspects of God needed an angel to act is Its vehicle of expression. To determine the names of these angels the angelic suffixes of IH or AL were added to each of the seventy-two names of God. The result became the seventy-two angels of the Shemhamphorash, the divided name of God.

These angels are assigned in pairs to the thirty-six decans of the zodiac and the thirty-six Small Cards of the tarot, beginning with the 5 of Wands – 0° Leo (again, the Chaldean start of the year). The names as they appear on the Small Cards of the *Tarot of Ceremonial Magick* are not the exact transliterations from Hebrew to English, but are traditional phonetic equivalents.

---

3. (v. 19) *And the angel of God, who went before the camp of Israel, moved and went behind them; and the pillar of the cloud moved from before them and stood behind them:* (v. 20) *And it came between the army of the Egyptians and the camp of Israel; and it was cloudy and dark all the night, but it gave light all the night to the children of Israel, so that they could not draw near one to another all the night.* (v. 21) *And Moses lifted up his hand over the sea; and the Lord caused the sea to go back by a strong east wind all that night and made the sea dry land, and the waters were divided.*

THE SEVENTY-TWO
SPIRITS OF THE GOETIA

Along with the Enochian information, the inclusion of the seventy-two spirits of the *Goetia* on the thirty-six Small Cards is perhaps the most significant feature of the *Tarot of Ceremonial Magick*. Never before have the correct attributions of these spirits been incorporated into a deck of Tarot cards. This information has been drawn from Aleister Crowley's qabalistic masterpiece, *777* [cols. 155–166].[4]

Goetic evocation is one of the most popular and widely practiced forms of Western ceremonial magick. The technique is classic; the magician stands within a magical circle protected by divine names. By means of pure will (and an appeal to higher spiritual powers), the magician evokes the spirit into a triangle outside of the circle. The magician then "charges" the spirit to perform some task which by tradition the spirit is known to be capable of performing. A more complete essay concerning Goetic evocation is found in Appendix Four of this book.

The seventy-two spirits of the *Goetia*[5] are taken from the first book of the *Lemegeton*, commonly called *The Lesser Key of Solomon*, and represent forces which in antiquity were considered "fallen angels." The modern magician, however, does not view these spirits in the same sinister light. Rather, they represent imbalanced and heretofore uncontrolled aspects of the magician him/herself, which, if properly called forth, controlled and directed, can be of immeasurable benefit, especially in mundane and material matters.

---

4. Aleister Crowley, *777 and Other Qabalistic Writings* (York Beach, ME: Samuel Weiser, 1990), pp. 28–33.
5. Goetia was originally a Greek word for sorcery or witchcraft (γοετεία). A related word *goetes* means "a wailer" and perhaps alludes to the long tradition of the sanctity of "barbarous names of evocation" extending back to classical times.

Like the seventy-two angels of the Shemhamphorash, the spirits of the *Goetia* are assigned to the thirty-six Small Cards in pairs, but unlike the angels of the Shemhamphorash each pair of Goetic spirits represents the entire ten degrees of their decan; one for the day (found on the lower left of each Small Card) and one for the night (found on the lower right.) Their names surround their seals are read by starting with the top letter and reading clockwise.

It should be pointed out that the attributes and correspondences of the Small Cards do not define the characteristics of the spirits of the Goetia or *vice versa*. The spirit *Orobas*, for example, is attributed to the night-time hours of the first ten degrees of Libra, and this period is represented in the tarot by the Two of Swords, PEACE RESTORED. This does not necessarily mean, however, that *Orobas* is characterized by the concept of PEACE RESTORED, or that *Orobas* can only be evoked between September 23 and October 2. It all depends on the question and how the cards are being utilized.

For example, let's say you have an appointment for an important job interview on the morning of August 12 and wish to know what to expect and what your basic attitude should be with the interviewer. You give yourself a simple tarot reading and receive the Two of Swords as your final card. This indicates the interview will most likely go well if you stress your ability to work well with others and avoid appearing disruptive or controversial.

Or ... on the night before your interview you wish to evoke a spirit of the Goetia to be your magical side-kick at the interview. You give yourself a tarot reading to determine which spirit would be appropriate for such a task and come up with the Two of Swords.[6] Of the two Goetic spirits on the card, *Orobas* seems the most appropriate, and so and so you evoke *Orobas* and carry his charged sigil with you to the interview.

---

6. If your answer is represented by a Trump, a Mercurial or Qliphothic spirit is appropriate; an Ace or Court Card, an Enochian spirit.

Or ... let's say that you have the same question but you also have control over the date your job interview will take place. This time the Two of Swords would not only give you the proper attitude but also the appropriate spirit and the date of the interview.

THE ENOCHIAN SQUARE
FROM THE GRAND CROSS
OF THE ELEMENTAL TABLETS

In the upper left-hand corner of each of the Small Cards is found a single Enochian Square. This square is taken from the Grand Cross section of each of the four Elemental Tablets. The Grand Cross is made up thirty-six squares arranged in two vertical columns intersected at their centers by one horizontal row. It is the Grand Cross which divides each Elemental Tablet into four subsections or "subangles."

The Grand Cross contains the names of seven very important angels in the Enochian system, the planetary Seniors. These angels, whose names must never be omitted in invocations of the Elemental Tablets, are located in the same positions on all four Tablets.

Each Grand Cross square displayed on the Small Cards includes the zodiacal and planetary attributes which characterize the Small Cards. There is no letter in the square as it appears on the card because this square occupies a different position in each of the four Elemental Tablets.

Example: The Two of Swords (first decan of Libra, Moon in Libra) is "N" on the Fire Tablet, "Z" on the Water Tablet, "f" on the Air Tablet, and "i" on the Earth Tablet.

The following tables show how the thirty-six Small Cards are placed on the four Elemental Tablets. By comparing these diagrams with the lettering on the tablets as they appear on the four Aces of the *Tarot of Ceremonial Magick* the appropriate letter for each element can be determined.

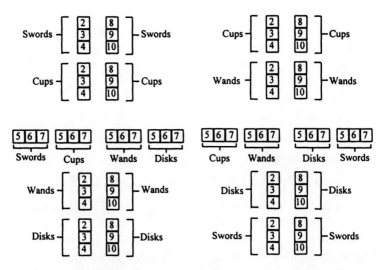

Figure 13.   Order of the Small Cards on the Enochian Tablet of Air.

Figure 14.   Order of the Small Cards on the Enochian Tablet of Water.

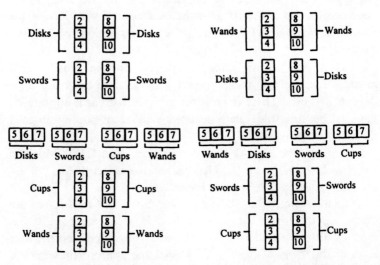

Figure 15.   Order of the Small Cards on the Enochian Tablet of Earth.

Figure 16.   Order of the Small Cards on the Enochian Tablet of Fire.

The positions of the seven planetary Seniors are shown in figure 17. The Sun Senior is also considered the Great King of the Elemental Tablet.

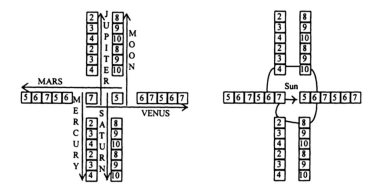

Figure 17. Positions of the Enochian Planetary Seniors. The name of the Great King or Sun Senior is determined by a clockwise whirl as shown above.

TWO OF WANDS
Dominion

0° to 10° Aries (March 21 to March 30)

Mars in Aries — Chokmah of Atziluth

Color: Pure soft blue.

General divinatory meanings: First manifestation of Fire. Ideal will, independent and creative. Control over circumstances.

Angels of the Shemhamphorash: VEHUEL (Great and Lofty) and DANIEL (Merciful Judge)

Day Spirit of the Goetia: #1, BAEL

A King ruling in the East; he maketh thee to go invisible, he ruleth over 66 Legions of Infernal Spirits. He appeareth in divers shapes, sometimes like a cat, sometimes like a toad, and sometimes like a man, and sometimes all these forms at once. He speaketh hoarsely.

Night Spirit of the Goetia: #37, PHENEX (or PHEYNIX)

He is a great Marquis, and appeareth like the bird Phoenix, having the voice of a child. He singeth many sweet notes before the Exorcist, which he must not regard, but by-and-by he must bid him put on human shape. Then will he speak marvelously of all wonderful sciences if required. He is a poet, good and excellent. And he will be willing to perform thy requests. He hath hopes also to return to the seventh throne after 1,200 years more, as he said unto Solomon. He governeth 20 Legions of Spirits.

Enochian Attributions — from Grand Cross of the Elemental Tablets (see Aces):

			Enochian	Senior	Temple Opening	Call
Air	V	of	baTai_V_Ah	King/Sun	2°=9°	#3
	V	of	A_V_ToTar	Mercury	2°=9°	#3
Water	i	of	sai_i_nou	Jupiter	3°= 8°	#4
Earth	i	of	ahml_i_cU	Mercury	1°=10°	#5
Fire	T	of	adoeoe_T_	Jupiter	4°=7°	#6

THREE OF WANDS
Established Strength

10° to 20° Aries (March 31 to April 10)

Sol in Aries — Binah of Atziluth

Color: Crimson.

General divinatory meanings: Success. Harmony following struggle.

Angels of the Shemhamphorash: HAHAZIAH (Secret, Impenetrable) and AMAMIAH (Covered in darkness)

Day Spirit of the Goetia: #2, AGARES (or AGREAS)

> He is under the power of the East, and cometh up in the form of an old fair man, riding upon a crocodile, carrying a goshawk upon his fist. He maketh them to run that stand still, and bringeth back runaways. He teaches all languages or tongues presently. He hath power also to destroy dignities both spiritual and temporal, and causeth earthquakes. He was of the order of Virtues. He hath under his government 31 Legions of Spirits.

Night Spirit of the Goetia: #38, HALPHAS (or MALTHUS, or MALTHAS)

> He is a great Earl, and appeareth in the form of a stock-dove. He speaketh with a hoarse voice. His office is to build up towers, and to furnish them with ammunition and weapons, and to send men-of-war to places appointed. He ruleth over 26 Legions of Spirits.

Enochian Attributions — from Grand Cross of the Elemental Tablets (see Aces):

			Enochian	Senior	Temple Opening	Call
Air	T	of	**AVToTar**	Mercury	2°=9°	#3
Water	i	of	**saiinou**	Jupiter	3°=8°	#4
Earth	c	of	**ahmlicU**	Mercury	1°=10°	#5
Fire	e	of	**adoeoeT**	Jupiter	4°=7°	#6

FOUR OF WANDS
Perfected Work

20° to 30° Aries (April 11 to April 20)

Venus in Aries — Chesed of Atziluth

Color: Deep violet.

General divinatory meanings: Completion. Order. Limitaion. By tact and gentleness a strived-for goal is achieved.

Angels of the Shemhamphorash: NANAEL (Caster down of the proud) and NITHAEL (Celestial King)

Day Spirit of the Goetia: #3, VASSAGO

A mighty Prince, being of the same nature as Agares. This Spirit is of a good nature, and his office is to declare things past and to come, and to discover all things hid or lost. And he governeth 26 Legions of Spirits.

Night Spirit of the Goetia: #39, MALPHAS

He appeareth at first like a crow, but after he will put on human shape at the request of the Exorcist, and speak with a hoarse voice. He is a mighty President and powerful. He can build houses and high towers, and can bring to thy knowledge enemies' desires and thoughts, and that which they have done. He giveth good familiars. If thou makest a sacrifice unto him he will receive it kindly and willingly, but he will deceive him that doth it. He governeth 40 Legions of Spirits.

Enochian Attributions — from Grand Cross of the Elemental Tablets (see Aces):

			Enochian	*Senior*	*Temple Opening*	*Call*
Air	o	of	AVToTar	Mercury	$2°=9°$	#3
Water	a	of	raagiosl	King/Sun	$3°=8°$	#4
	a	of	saiinou	Jupiter	$3°=8°$	#4
Earth	U	of	ahmlicU	Mercury	$1°=10°$	#5
Fire	o	of	adoeoeT	Jupiter	$4°=7°$	#6

FIVE OF WANDS

Strife

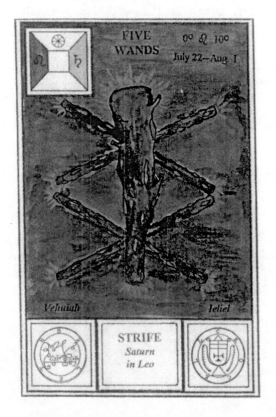

0° to 10° Leo (July 22 to August 1)

Saturn in Leo — Geburah of Atziluth

Color: Orange.

General divinatory meanings: Stress. Destruction. Purgation preceding renewal. Conflict. Quarrelling. Vigorous, even violent belligerency.

Angels of the Shemhamphorash: VEHUIAH (God the exalter) and IELIEL (Strength)

Day Spirit of the Goetia: #13, BELETH (or BILETH, or BILET)

> He is a mighty King and terrible. He rideth on a pale horse with trumpets and other kinds of musical instruments playing before him. He is very furious at his first appearance, that is, while the Exorcist layeth his courage; for to do this he must hold a hazel wand in his hand, striking it out towards the South and East quarters, make a triangle, △, without the circle, and then command him into it by the bonds and charges of Spirits as hereafter followeth. And if he doth not enter into the triangle, △, at your threats, rehearse the bonds and charms before him, and then he will yield obedience and come into it, and do what he is commanded by the Exorcist. Yet he must receive him courteously because he is a great King, and do homage unto him, as the Kings and Princes do that attend upon him. And thou must have always a silver ring in the middle finger or the left hand held against thy face, as they do yet before Amaymon. This great King Beleth causeth all the love that may be, both of men and of women, until the Master Exorcist hath had his desire fulfilled. He is of the order of Powers, and he governeth 85 Legions of Spirits.

Night Spirit of the Goetia: #49, CROCELL (or CROKEL)

> He appeareth in the form of an angel. He is a Duke great and strong, speaking something mystically of hidden things. He teacheth the art of geometry and the liberal sciences. He, at the command of the Exorcist will produce great noises like the rushings of many waters, although there be none. He warmeth waters, and discovereth baths. He was of the order of Potestates, or Powers, before his fall, as he declared unto the King Solomon. He governeth 48 Legions of Spirits.

Enochian Attributions — from Grand Cross of the Elemental Tablets (see Aces):

		Enochian	*Senior*	*Temple Opening*	*Call*
Air	h	of baTaiVA<u>h</u>	King/Sun	2°=9°	#3
	h	of A<u>h</u>aozpi	Venus	2°=9°	#3
	h	of <u>h</u>Abioro	Mars	2°=9°	#3
	h	of hTmordA	Moon	2°=9°	#3
	h	of <u>h</u>ipotga	Saturn	2°=9°	#3
Water	a	of lsr<u>a</u>hpm	Mars	3°=8°	#4
Earth	t	of alhC<u>t</u>Ga	Venus	1°=10°	#5
Fire	o	of aaetPi<u>o</u>	Mars	4°=7°	#6

SIX OF WANDS

Victory

10° to 20° Leo (August 2 to August 11)

Jupiter in Leo — Tiphareth of Atziluth

Color: Clear pink rose.

General divinatory meanings: Exultation after struggle. Harmony. Beauty. Stability. Perfect balance. Accomplishment. Gain.

Angels of the Shemhamphorash: SITAEL (Refuge, Fortress) and ELEMIAH (Concealed, Deliverance)

Day Spirit of the Goetia: #14, LERAIE (or LERAJE, or LERAIKHA)

He is a Marquis great in power, showing himself in the likeness of an archer clad in green, and carrying a bow and quiver. He causeth all great battles and contests; and maketh wounds to putrefy that are made with arrows by archers. This belongeth unto Sagittary. He governeth 30 Legions of Spirits.

Night Spirit of the Goetia: #50, FURCAS

He is a Knight, and appeareth in the form of a cruel old man with a long beard and a hoary head, riding upon a pale-coloured horse, with a sharp weapon in his hand. His office is to teach the arts of philosophy, astrology, rhetoric, logic, cheiromancy, and pyromancy, in all their parts, and perfectly. He hath under his power 20 Legions of Spirits.

Enochian Attributions — from Grand Cross of the Elemental Tablets (see Aces):

			Enochian	Senior	Temple Opening	Call
Air	a	of	Ah̲aozpi	Venus	$2°=9°$	#3
Water	r	of	r̲aagiosl	King/Sun	$3°=8°$	#4
	r	of	ls̲rahpm	Mars	$3°=8°$	#4
Earth	G	of	alhCtG̲a	Venus	$1°=10°$	#5
Fire	i	of	aaetP̲io	Mars	$4°=7°$	#6

SEVEN OF WANDS

Valour

20° to 30° Leo (August 12 to August 22)

Mars in Leo—Netzach of Atziluth

Color: Amber.

General divinatory meanings: Equilibrium disturbed. Loss of confidence. Difficulties requiring courage and tenacity to overcome.

Angels of the Shemhamphorash: MAHASIAH (Seeking deliverance from fears) and LELAHEL (Sing praises)

Day Spirit of the Goetia: #15, ELIGOS

> He is a great Duke, and appeareth in the form of a goodly knight, carrying a lance, an ensign, and a serpent. He discovereth hidden things, and knoweth things to come; and of wars, and how the soldiers will or shall meet. He causeth the love of lords and great persons. He governeth 60 Legions of Spirits.

Night Spirit of the Goetia: #51, BALAM

> He is a terrible, great, and powerful King. He appeareth with three heads: the first is like that of a bull; the second is like that of a man; the third is like that of a ram. He hath the tail of a serpent, and flaming eyes. He rideth upon a furious bear, and carrieth a goshawk upon his fist. He speaketh with a hoarse voice, giving true answers of things past, present, and to come. He maketh men to go invisible, and also to be witty. He governeth 40 Legions of Spirits.

Enochian Attributions—from Grand Cross of the Elemental Tablets (see Aces):

			Enochian	*Senior*	*Temple Opening*	*Call*
Air	o	of	Aha_ozpi	Venus	2°=9°	#3
Water	s	of	raagio_sl	King/Sun	3°=8°	#4
	s	of	l_srahpm	Mars	3°=8°	#4
	s	of	_soniznt	Mercury	3°=8°	#4
	s	of	_saiinou	Jupiter	3°=8°	#4
	s	of	_slgoiol	Venus	3°=8°	#4
Earth	a	of	alhCtG_a	Venus	1°=10°	#5
Fire	P	of	aaet_Pio	Mars	4°=7°	#6

EIGHT OF WANDS

Swiftness

0° to 10° Sagittarius. (November 23 to December 2)

Mercury in Sagittarius — Hod of Atziluth

Color: Violet purple.

General divinatory meanings: Sudden flash of activity; too much too soon. Speech. Electricity. A telephone call, letter, or message.

Angels of the Shemhamphorash: NITHHAIAH (Wonderworking) and HAAIAH (Heaven in secret)

Day Spirit of the Goetia: #25, GLASYA-LABOLAS

He is a mighty President and Earl, and showeth himself in the form of a dog with wings like a gryphon. He teacheth all arts and sciences in an instant, and is an author of bloodshed and manslaughter. He teacheth all things past, and to come. If desired he causeth the love both of friends and of foes. He can make a man to go invisible. And he hath under his command 36 Legions of Spirits.

Night Spirit of the Goetia: #61, ZAGAN

He is a great King and President, appearing at first in the form of a bull with gryphon's wings; but after a while he putteth on human shape. He maketh men witty. He can turn wine into water, and blood into wine, also water into wine. He can turn all metals into coin of the dominion that metal is of. He can even make fools wise. He governeth 33 Legions of Spirits.

Enochian Attributions — from Grand Cross of the Elemental Tablets (see Aces):

			Enochian	*Senior*	*Temple Opening*	*Call*
Air	i	of	baTaiVAh	King/Sun	2°=9°	#3
	i	of	hipotga	Saturn	2°=9°	#3
Water	a	of	laoaxrp	Moon	3°=8°	#4
Earth	n	of	liiansa	Saturn	1°=10°	#5
Fire	d	of	aLndUod	Mars	4°=7°	#6

NINE OF WANDS

Great Strength

10° to 20° Sagittarius. (December 3 to December 12)

Moon in Sagittarius — Yesod of Atziluth

Color: Indigo.

General divinatory meanings: Recovered balance and health. Success follows struggle. Change is stability.

Angels of the Shemhamphorash: IEATHEL (Deliver) and SAHIIAH (Remover of evils)

Day Spirit of the Goetia: #26, BUNÉ (or BIMÉ) or BIM

> He is a strong, great and mighty Duke. He appeareth in the form of a dragon with three heads, one like a dog, one like gryphon, and one like a man. He speaketh with a high and comely voice. He changeth the place of the dead, and causeth the Spirits which be under him to gather together upon your sepulchres. He giveth riches unto a man, and maketh him wise and eloquent. He giveth true answers unto demands and he governeth 30 Legions of Spirits.

Night Spirit of the Goetia: #62, VALAC (or VOLAC, or VALAK, or VALU, or UALAC)

> He is a President mighty and great, and appeareth like a child with angel's wings, riding on a two-headed dragon. His office is to give true answers of hidden treasures, and to tell where serpents may be seen. The which he will bring unto the Exorciser without any force or strength being by him employed. He governeth 38 Legions of Spirits.

Enochian Attributions — from Grand Cross of the Elemental Tablets (see Aces):

			Enochian	*Senior*	*Temple Opening*	*Call*
Air	p	of	hipotga	Saturn	$2°=9°$	#3
Water	o	of	laoaxrp	Moon	$3°=8°$	#4
Earth	s	of	liiansa	Saturn	$1°=10°$	#5
Fire	o	of	aLndUod	Moon	$4°=7°$	#6

TEN OF WANDS

Oppression

20° to 30° Sagittarius. (December 13 to December 21)

Saturn in Sagittarius — Malkuth of Atziluth

Color: Yellow.

General divinatory meanings: Blind force. Violent energy. Obstinate cruelty. Self devouring lust of result.

Angels of the Shemhamphorash: REIIEL (Expectation) and AMAEL (Patience)

Day Spirit of the Goetia: #27, RONOVÉ

He appeareth in the form of a monster. He teacheth the art of rhetoric very well, and giveth good servants, knowledge of tongues, and favours with friends or foes. He is a Marquis and great Earl; and there be under his command 19 Legions of Spirits.

Night Spirit of the Goetia: #63, ANDRAS

He is a great Marquis, appearing in the form of an angel with a head like a black night raven, riding upon a strong black wolf, and having a sharp and bright sword flourished aloft in his hand. His office is to sow discords. If the Exorcist have not a care, he will slay both him and his fellows. He governeth 30 Legions of Spirits.

Enochian Attributions—from Grand Cross of the Elemental Tablets (see Aces):

			Enochian	*Senior*	*Temple Opening*	*Call*
Air	o	of	hip̲o̲tga	Saturn	$2°=9°$	#3
Water	a	of	ra̲a̲giosl	King/Sun	$3°=8°$	#4
	a	of	la̲o̲axrp	Moon	$3°=8°$	#4
Earth	a	of	liiansa̲	Saturn	$1°=10°$	#5
Fire	U	of	aLndU̲od	Moon	$4°=7°$	#6

TWO OF CUPS

Love

0° to 10° Cancer (June 21 to July 1)

Venus in Cancer — Chokmah of Briah

Color: Gray.

General divinatory meanings: First manifestation of water. Perfect harmony between male and female. Ecstasy. Joy.

Angels of the Shemhamphorash: EIAEL (Delights of the Sons of men) and HABUIAH (Great benefactor)

Day Spirit of the Goetia: #10, BUER

> He is a great President. He appeareth in Sagittary, and that is his shape when the Sun is there. He teaches philosophy, both moral and natural, and the logic art, and also the virtues of all herbs and plants. He healeth all distempers in man, and giveth good familiars.

Night Spirit of the Goetia: #46, BIFRONS (or BIFFRÖUS, or BIFROVS)

> He is an Earl, and appeareth in the form of a monster; but after a while, at the command of the Exorcist, he putteth on the shape of a man. His office is to make one knowing in astrology, geometry, and other arts and sciences. He teacheth the virtues of precious stones and woods. He changeth dead bodies, and putteth them in another place; also he lighteth seeming candles upon the graves of the dead. He hath under his command 60 Legions of Spirits.

Enochian Attributions — from Grand Cross of the Elemental Tablets (see Aces):

			Enochian	Senior	Temple Opening	Call
Air	z	of	Aaozaif	Jupiter	2°=9°	#3
Water	u	of	saiinou	Jupiter	3°=8°	#4
Earth	h	of	iCZhihal	King/Sun	1°=10°	#5
	h	of	ahmlicU	Mercury	1°=10°	#5
Fire	o	of	aNodoin	Mercury	4°=7°	#6

THREE OF CUPS

Abundance

10° to 20° Cancer (July 2 to July 11)

Mercury in Cancer — Binah of Briah

Color: Black.

General divinatory meanings: Love bares fruit. Bounty. Enjoy but mistrust the good things in life.

Angels of the Shemhamphorash: ROCHEL (All-seeing) and
IIBAMIAH (Creating by His Word)

Day Spirit of the Goetia: #11, GUSION

A great and strong Duke. He appeareth like a Xenopilus.[5] He telleth all
things, past, present, and to come, and showeth the meaning and reso-
lution of all questions thou mayest ask. He conciliated and reconcileth
friendships, and giveth honour and dignity unto any. He ruleth over 40
Legions of Spirits.

Night Spirit of the Goetia: #47, VUAL (or UVALL, or VOVAL)

He is a Duke, great, mighty, and strong; and appeareth in the form of
a mighty dromedary at the first, but after a while at the command of
the Exorcist he putteth on human shape, and speaketh the Egyptian
tongue, but not perfectly. His office is to procure the love of women,
and to tell things past, present, and to come. He also procureth friendship between friends and foes. He was of the order of Potestates or
Powers. He governeth 37 Legions of Spirits.

Enochian Attributions — from Grand Cross of the Elemental Tablets (see Aces):

			Enochian	Senior	Temple Opening	Call
Air	o	of	Aaozaif	Jupiter	2°=9°	#3
Water	o	of	saiinou	Jupiter	3°=8°	#4
Earth	m	of	ahmlicU	Mercury	1°=10°	#5
Fire	i	of	aNodoin	Mercury	4°=7°	#6

---

5. Blue-headed or strange-headed creature.

FOUR OF CUPS
Blended Pleasure

20° to 30° Cancer (July 12 to July 21)

Moon in Cancer — Chesed of Briah

Color: Blue.

General divinatory meanings: Luxury. Seed of the decay of pleasure. Weakness, surrender to desire.

Angels of the Shemhamphorash: HAIAIEL (Lord of the Universe) and MUMIAH (End of the Universe)

Day Spirit of the Goetia: #12, SITRI

He is a great Prince, and appeareth at first with a leopard's head and the wings of a gryphon, but after the command of the Master of the Exorcism he putteth on human shape, and that very beautiful. He enflameth men with women's love, and women with men's love; and causeth them also to show themselves naked if it be desired. He governeth 60 Legions of Spirits.

Night Spirit of the Goetia: #48, HAAGENTI

He is a President, appearing in the form of a mighty bull with gryphon's wings. This is at first, but after, at the command of the Exorcist he putteth on human shape. His office is to make men wise, and to instruct them in divers things; also to transmute all metals into gold; and to change wine into water, and water into wine. He governeth 33 Legions of Spirits.

Enochian Attributions — from Grand Cross of the Elemental Tablets (see Aces):

			Enochian	Senior	Temple Opening	Call
Air	a	of	ba̱TaiVAh	King/Sun	2°=9°	#3
	a	of	Aa̱ozaif	Jupiter	2°=9°	#3
Water	n	of	saii̱nou	Jupiter	3°=8°	#4
Earth	1	of	ahmḻicU	Mercury	1°=10°	#5
Fire	n	of	aNodoi̱n	Mercury	4°=7°	#6

FIVE OF CUPS

Loss in Pleasure

0° to 10° Scorpio (October 23 to November 1)

Mars in Scorpio — Geburah of Briah

Color: Scarlet red.

General divinatory meanings: Disappointment in love or pleasure. Expected pleasure thwarted.

Angels of the Shemhamphorash: LEUUIAH (Hastening to hear) and PAHLIAH (Liberator from deceit)

Day Spirit of the Goetia: #22, IPOS

> He is an Earl, and a mighty prince, and appeareth in the form of an angel with a lion's head, and a goose's foot, and hare's tail. He knoweth all things past, present and to come. He maketh men witty and bold. He governeth 36 Legions of Spirits.

Night Spirit of the Goetia: #58, AMY (or AVNAS)

> He is a great President, and appeareth at first in the form of a flaming fire; but after a while he putteth on the shape of a Man. His office is to make one wonderful knowing in astrology and all the liberal sciences. He giveth good familiars, and can bewray treasure that is kept by Spirits. He governeth 36 Legions of Spirits.

Enochian Attributions—from Grand Cross of the Elemental Tablets (see Aces):

			Enochian	*Senior*	*Temple Opening*	*Call*
Air	i	of	hAbioro	Mars	2°=9°	#3
Water	m	of	lsrahpm	Mars	3°=8°	#4
Earth	1	of	iCZhihal	King/Sun	1°=10°	#5
	1	of	alhCtGa	Venus	1°=10°	#5
	1	of	lZinoPo	Moon	1°=10°	#5
	1	of	liiansa	Saturn	1°=10°	#5
	1	of	laidrOM	Mars	1°=10°	#5
Fire	o	of	aapDoce	Venus	4°=7°	#6

SIX OF CUPS

Pleasure

10° to 20° Scorpio (November 2 to November 12)

Sol in Scorpio — Tiphareth of Briah

Color: Yellow (gold).

General divinatory meanings: Harmony. Ease. Fertility. Not the gratification of artificial desires, but the fulfillment of the true sexual will. One of the best cards in the deck.

Angels of the Shemhamphorash: NELCHAEL (Thou alone) and IEIAIEL (Thy right hand)

Day Spirit of the Goetia: #23, AIM

He is a great strong Duke. He appeareth in the form of a very handsome man in body, but with three heads; the first, like a serpent, the second like a man having two stars on his forehead, the third like a calf. He rideth on a viper, carrying a firebrand in his hand, wherewith he setteth cities, castles, and great places on fire. He maketh thee witty in all manner of ways, and giveth true answers unto private matters. He governeth 26 Legions of Inferior Spirits.

Night Spirit of the Goetia: #59, ORIAS (or ORIAX)

He is a Great Marquis, and appeareth with the face of a lion, riding upon a horse mighty and strong, with a serpent's tail; and he holdeth in his right hand two great serpents hissing. His office is to teach the virtues of the stars, and to know the mansions of the planets, and how to understand their virtues. He also transformeth men, and he giveth dignities, prelacies, and confirmation thereof; also favour with friends and with foes. He doth govern 30 Legions of Spirits.

Enochian Attributions — from Grand Cross of the Elemental Tablets (see Aces):

			Enochian	Senior	Temple Opening	Call
Air	b	of	baTaiVAh	King/Sun	2°=9°	#3
	b	of	hAbioro	Mars	2°=9°	#3
Water	p	of	lsrahpm	Mars	3°=8°	#4
Earth	h	of	alhCtGa	Venus	1°=10°	#5
Fire	c	of	aapDoce	Venus	4°=7°	#6

SEVEN OF CUPS
Illusionary Success

20° to 30° Scorpio (November 13 to November 22)

Venus in Scorpio — Netzach of Briah

Color: Emerald.

General divinatory meanings: Debauch. Addiction. False pleasure. External splendour, internal corruption. Guilt. Deception.

Angels of the Shemhamphorash: MELAHEL (Repelling evil) and HAHUIAH (Trusting in Him)

Day Spirit of the Goetia: #24, NABERIUS

He is a most valiant Marquis, and showeth in the form of a black crane fluttering about the circle, and when he speaketh it is with a hoarse voice. He maketh men cunning in all arts and sciences, but especially in the art of rhetoric. He restoreth lost dignities and honours. He governeth 19 Legions of Spirits.

Night Spirit of the Goetia: #60, VAPULA (or NAPHULA)

He is a Duke great, mighty, and strong; appearing in the form of a lion with gryphon's wings. His office is to make men knowing in all handicrafts and professions, also in philosophy, and other sciences. He governeth 36 Legions of Spirits.

Enochian Attributions—from Grand Cross of the Elemental Tablets (see Aces):

			Enochian	*Senior*	*Temple Opening*	*Call*
Air	A	of	baTaiVAh	King/Sun	$2° = 9°$	#3
	A	of	hAbioro	Mars	$2° = 9°$	#3
	A	of	AVToTar	Mercury	$2° = 9°$	#3
	A	of	Ahaozpi	Venus	$2° = 9°$	#3
	A	of	Aaozaif	Jupiter	$2° = 9°$	#3
Water	h	of	lsrahpm	Mars	$3° = 8°$	#4
Earth	C	of	alhCtGa	Venus	$1° = 10°$	#5
Fire	e	of	aapDoce	Venus	$4° = 7°$	#6

EIGHT OF CUPS

Abandoned Success

0° to 10° Pisces (February 19 to February 28)

Saturn in Pisces — Hod of Briah

Color: Orange.

General divinatory meanings: Indolence. Unpleasantness. Sorrow plagues pleasure.

Angels of the Shemhamphorash: VEVALIAH (King and Ruler) and IELAHIAH (Abiding for ever)

Day Spirit of the Goetia: #34, FURFUR

> He is a great and mighty Earl, appearing in the form of an hart with a fiery tail. He never speaketh truth unless he be compelled, or brought up within a triangle Δ. Being therein, he will take upon himself the form of an angel. Being bidden, he speaketh with a hoarse voice. Also he will wittingly urge love between man and woman. He can raise lightnings and thunders, blasts, and great tempestuous storms. And he giveth true answers both of things secret and divine, if commanded. He ruleth over 26 Legions of Spirits.

Night Spirit of the Goetia: #70, SEERE (or SEAR, or SEIR)

> He is a mighty Prince, and powerful, under Amaymon, King of the East. He appeareth in the form of a beautiful man, riding upon a winged horse. His office is to go and come; and to bring abundance of things to pass on a sudden, and to carry or re-carry anything whither thou wouldest have it to go, or whence thou wouldest have it from. He can pass over the whole earth in the twinkling of an eye. He giveth a true relation of all sorts of theft, and of treasure hid, and of many other things. He is of an indifferent good nature, and is willing to do anything which the Exorcist desireth. He governeth 26 Legions of Spirits.

Enochian Attributions — from Grand Cross of the Elemental Tablets (see Aces):

		Enochian	Senior	Temple Opening	Call
Air	o	of hTm<u>o</u>rda	Moon	$2°=9°$	#3
Water	p	of laoaxr<u>p</u>	Moon	$3°=8°$	#4
Earth	i	of iCZh<u>i</u>hal	King/Sun	$1°=10°$	#5
	i	of l<u>ii</u>ansa	Saturn	$1°=10°$	#5
Fire	n	of ari<u>nn</u>A [6]	Saturn	$4°=7°$	#6

---

6. Dee and Kelley were directed by the communicating angels to inscribe several of the letters of the Elemental Tablets backwards. These reversed letters, ꟻAЯAOИ, form the name of the great Governor of the Second Division of the Twenty-Second Æthyr, *Lin.*

NINE OF CUPS
Material Happiness

10° to 20° Pisces (March 1 to March 10)

Jupiter in Pisces — Yesod of Briah

Color: Violet.

General divinatory meanings: Good fortune. Joy. Gladness. Self-fulfillment.

Angels of the Shemhamphorash: SALIAH (Mover of all things) and ARIEL (Revealer)

Day Spirit of the Goetia: #35, MARCHOSIAS

He is a great and mighty Marquis, appearing at first in the form of a wolf having gryphon's wings, and a serpent's tail, and vomiting fire out of his mouth. But after a time, at the command of the Exorcist he putteth on the shape of a man. And he is a strong fighter. He was of the order of Dominations. He governeth 30 Legions of Spirits. He told his Chief, who was Solomon, that after 1,200 years he had hopes to return unto the Seventh Throne.

Night Spirit of the Goetia: #71, DANTALION

He is a Duke great and mighty, appearing in the form of a man with many countenances, all men's and women's faces; and he hath a book in his right hand. His office is to teach all arts and sciences unto any; and to declare the secret counsels of anyone; for he knoweth the thoughts of all men and women, and can change them at his will. He can cause love, and show the similitude of any person, and show the same by a vision, let them be in what part of the world they will. He governeth 36 Legions of Spirits.

Enochian Attributions — from Grand Cross of the Elemental Tablets (see Aces):

			Enochian	Senior	Temple Opening	Call
Air	m	of	hTmorda	Moon	2°=9°	#3
Water	r	of	laoaxrp	Moon	3°=8°	#4
Earth	i	of	lijansa	Saturn	1°=10°	#5
Fire	A	of	arinnA	Saturn	4°=7°	#6

TEN OF CUPS

Perfected Success

20° to 30° Pisces (March 11 to March 20)

Mars in Pisces — Malkuth of Briah

Colors: Citrine, Olive, Russet, and Black.

General divinatory meanings: Satiety. One's cup runneth over and stains the carpet.

Angels of the Shemhamphorash: ASALIAH (Just judge) and MIHAEL (Sending forth as a father)

Day Spirit of the Goetia: #36, STOLAS (or STOLOS)

> He is a great and powerful Prince, appearing in the shape of a mighty raven at first before the Exorcist; but after he taketh the image of a man. He teacheth the art of astronomy, and virtues of herbs and precious stones. He governeth 26 Legions of Spirits.

Night Spirit of the Goetia: #72, ANDROMALIUS

> He is an Earl, great and mighty, appearing in the form of a man holding a great serpent in his hand. His office is to bring back both a thief, and the goods which be stolen; and to discover all wickedness, and underhand dealing; and to punish all thieves and other wicked people; and also to discover treasures that be hid. He ruleth over 36 Legions of Spirits.

Enochian Attributions—from Grand Cross of the Elemental Tablets (see Aces):

			Enochian	Senior	Temple Opening	Call
Air	T	of	baTaiVAh	King/Sun	2°=9°	#3
	T	of	hTmorda	Moon	2°=9°	#3
Water	x	of	laoaxrp	Moon	3°=8°	#4
Earth	a	of	liiansa	Saturn	1°=10°	#5
Fire		of	arinnA_	Saturn	4°=7°	#6

TWO OF SWORDS

Peace Restored

0° to 10° Libra (September 23 to October 2)

Moon in Libra — Chokmah of Yetzirah

Color: Blue pearl gray (mother-of-pearl).

General divinatory meanings: First manifestation of air. Equilibrium abiding above disruption. Dormant antagonism.

Angels of the Shemhamphorash: IEIAZEL (Rejoicing over all) and MEBAHEL (Guardian and preserver)

Day Spirit of the Goetia: #19, SALLOS (or SALEOS)

He is a great and mighty Duke, and appeareth in the form of a gallant soldier riding on a crocodile, with a ducal crown on his head, but peaceably. He causeth the love of women to men, and of men to women; and governeth 30 Legions of Spirits.

Night Spirit of the Goetia: #55, OROBAS

He is a great and mighty Prince, appearing at first like a horse; but after the command of the Exorcist he putteth on the image of a man. His office is to discover all things past, present, and to come; also to give dignities, and prelacies, and the favour of friends and foes. He giveth true answers of divinity, and of the creation of the world. He is very faithful unto the Exorcist, and will not suffer him to be tempted of any Spirit. He governeth 20 Legions of Spirits.

Enochian Attributions—from Grand Cross of the Elemental Tablets (see Aces):

			Enochian	*Senior*	*Temple Opening*	*Call*
Air	f	of	Aaozaif	Jupiter	$2°=9°$	#3
Water	z	of	soni<u>z</u>nt	Mercury	$3°=8°$	#4
Earth	i	of	aCZ<u>i</u>noR	Jupiter	$1°=10°$	#5
Fire	N	of	edLpr<u>N</u>aa	King/Sun	$4°=7°$	#6
	N	of	a<u>N</u>odoin	Mercury	$4°=7°$	#6

THREE OF SWORDS

Sorrow

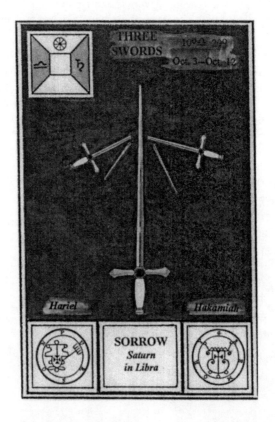

10° to 20° Libra (October 3 to October 12)

Saturn in Libra—Binah of Yetzirah

Color: Dark brown.

General divinatory meanings: Profound melancholy engendering either depression or wisdom. Secrecy. Perversion.

Angels of the Shemhamphorash: HARIEL (Aid) and HAKAMIAH (Arise, praying day and night)

Day Spirit of the Goetia: #20, PURSON

He is a great King. His appearing is comely, like a man with a lion's face, carrying a cruel viper in his hand, and riding upon a bear. Going before him are many trumpets sounding. He knoweth all things hidden, and can discover treasure, and tell all things past, present, and to come. He can take a body either human or aerial, and answereth truly of all earthly things both secret and divine, and of the creation of the world. He bringeth forth good familiars, and under his government there be 22 Legions of Spirits, partly of the order of Virtues and partly of the order of Thrones.

Night Spirit of the Goetia: #56 GREMORY (or GAMORI)

He is a Duke strong and powerful, and appeareth in the form of a beautiful woman, with a duchess's crown tied about her waist, and riding on a great camel. His office is to tell of all things past, present, and to come; and of treasures hid, and what they lie in; and to procure the love of women both young and old. He governeth 26 Legions of Spirits.

Enochian Attributions — from Grand Cross of the Elemental Tablets (see Aces):

			Enochian	*Senior*	*Temple Opening*	*Call*
Air	i	of	Aaozaif	Jupiter	$2°=9°$	#3
Water	n	of	soniznt	Mercury	$3°=8°$	#4
Earth	Z	of	aCZinoR	Jupiter	$1°=10°$	#5
Fire	o	of	aNodoin	Mercury	$4°=7°$	#6

FOUR OF SWORDS
Rest from Strife

20° to 30° Libra (October 13 to October 22)

Jupiter in Libra—Chesed of Yetzirah

Color: Deep purple.

General divinatory meanings: Truce. Compromise. Tension is relaxed through submission to militaristic discipline and dogma. Refuge from sorrow.

Angels of the Shemhamphorash: LEVIAH (Is wonderful) and CALIEL (Only unto me.)

Day Spirit of the Goetia: #21, MARAX

He is a great Earl and President. He appeareth like a great bull with a man's face. His office is to make men very knowing in astronomy, and all other liberal sciences; also he can give good familiars, and (is) wise, knowing the virtues of herbs and stones which be precious. He governeth 30 Legions of Spirits.

Night Spirit of the Goetia: #57, OSÉ (or OSO, or VOSO)

He is a great President, and appeareth like a leopard at the first, but after a little time he putteth on the shape of a man. His office is to make one cunning in the liberal sciences, and to give true answers of divine and secret things; also to change a man into any shape that the Exorcist pleaseth, so that he that is so changed will not think any other thing than that he is in verity that creature or thing his is changed into. He governeth 30 Legions of Spirits.

Enochian Attributions — from Grand Cross of the Elemental Tablets (see Aces):

			Enochian	Senior	Temple Opening	Call
Air	a	of	Aaoza̲if	Jupiter	2°=9°	#3
Water	t	of	sonizn̲t	Mercury	3°=8°	#4
Earth	C	of	iC̲Zhihal	King/Sun	1°=10°	#5
	C	of	aC̲ZinoR	Jupiter	1°=10°	#5
Fire	d	of	aNod̲oin	Mercury	4°=7°	#6

FIVE OF SWORDS

Defeat

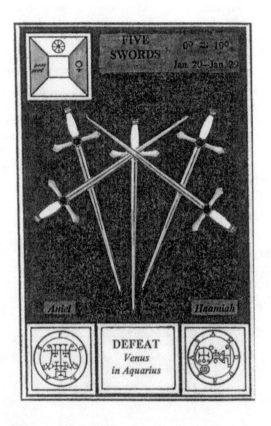

0° to 10° Aquarius (January 20 to January 29)

Venus in Aquarius — Geburah of Yetzirah

Color: Bright scarlet.

General divinatory meanings: Failure. Inadequate energy to maintain peace. Reason is undone by sentiment.

Angels of the Shemhamphorash: ANIEL (Lord of Virtues) and HAAMIAH (Hope of all the Earth)

Day Spirit of the Goetia: #31, FORAS

> He is a mighty President, and appeareth in the form of a strong man in human shape. He can give the understanding to men how they may know the virtues of all herbs and precious stones. He teacheth the arts of logic and ethics in all their parts. If desired he maketh men invisible, and to live long, and to be eloquent. He can discover treasures and recover things lost. He ruleth over 29 Legions of Spirits.

Night Spirit of the Goetia: #67, AMDUSIAS (or AMDUKIAS)

> He is a Duke great and strong, appearing at first like a unicorn, but at the request of the Exorcist he standeth before him in human shape, causing trumpets, and all manner of musical instruments to be heard, but not soon or immediately. Also he can cause trees to bend and incline according the Exorcist's will. He giveth excellent familiars. He governeth 29 Legions of Spirits.

Enochian Attributions — from Grand Cross of the Elemental Tablets (see Aces):

			Enochian	*Senior*	*Temple Opening*	*Call*
Air	o	of	hAbioro	Mars	2°=9°	#3
Water	i	of	slgaiol	Venus	3°=8°	#4
Earth	d	of	laidrOM	Mars	1°=10°	#5
Fire	a	of	edLprNaa	King/Sun	4°=7°	#6
	a	of	aapDoce	Venus	4°=7°	#6
	a	of	arinnA	Saturn	4°=7°	#6
	a	of	aaetPio	Mars	4°=7°	#6
	a	of	aLndUod	Moon	4°=7°	#6

SIX OF SWORDS
Earned Success

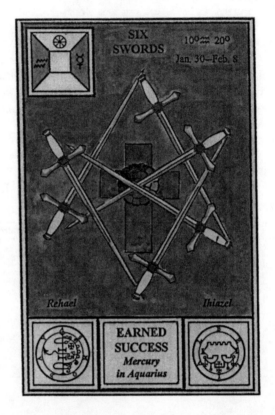

10° to 20° Aquarius (January 30 to February 8)

Mercury in Aquarius — Tiphareth of Yetzirah

Color: Rich salmon.

General divinatory meanings: Intellectual endeavors rewarded. Equilibrium of mental and moral faculties. "The method of science, the aim of religion."

Angels of the Shemhamphorash: REHAEL (Swift to condone) and IHIAZEL (Making joyful)

Day Spirit of the Goetia: #32, ASMODAY (or ASMODAI)

He is a great King, strong, and powerful. He appeareth with three heads, whereof the first is like a bull, the second like a man, and the third like a Ram; he hath also the tail of a serpent, and from his mouth issue flames of fire. His feet are webbed like those of a goose. He sitteth upon an infernal dragon, and beareth in his hand a lance with a banner. He is first and choicest under the Power of Amaymon, he goeth before all other. When the Exorcist hath a mind to call him, let it be abroad, and let him stand on his feet all the time of action, with his cap or head-dress off; for if it be on Amaymon will deceive him and call all his actions to bewrayed. But as soon as the Exorcist seeth Asmoday in the shape aforesaid, he shall call him by his name, saying: "Art thou Asmoday?" and he will not deny it, and by-and-by he will bow down unto the ground. He giveth the Ring of Virtues; he teacheth the arts of arithmetic, astronomy, geometry, and all handicrafts absolutely. He giveth true and full answers unto thy demands. He maketh one invincible. He showeth the place where treasures lie, and guardeth it. He, amongst the Legions of Amaymon governeth 72 Legions of Spirits Inferior.

Night Spirit of the Goetia: #68, BELIAL

He is a mighty and a powerful King, and was created next after Lucifer. He appeareth in the form of two beautiful angels sitting in a chariot of fire. He speaketh with a comely voice, and declareth that he fell first from among the worthier sort, that were before Michael, and other heavenly angels. His office is distribute presentations and Senatorships, etc., and to cause favour or friends and foes. He giveth excellent familiars, and governeth 50 Legions of Spirits. Note well that this King Belial must have offerings sacrifices and gifts presented unto him by the Exorcist, or else he will not give true answers unto his demands. But he tarrieth not one hour in the truth, unless he be constrained by divine power.

Enochian Attributions — from Grand Cross of the Elemental Tablets (see Aces):

			Enochian	*Senior*	*Temple Opening*	*Call*
Air	r	of	hAbioro	Mars	$2°=9°$	#3
Water	o	of	slgaiol	Venus	$3°=8°$	#4
Earth	i	of	laidrOM	Mars	$1°=10°$	#5
Fire	p	of	edLprNaa	King/Sun	$4°=7°$	#6
	p	of	aapDoce	Venus	$4°=7°$	#6

SEVEN OF SWORDS
Unstable Effort

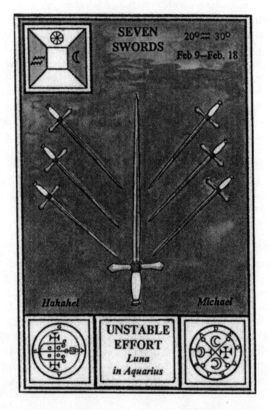

20° to 30° Aquarius (February 9 to February 18)

Moon in Aquarius — Netzach of Yetzirah

Color: Bright yellow-green.

General divinatory meanings: Futility. Indecisiveness. Appease-
ment. Swimming against the tide. Insufficient energy and will to
complete the task.

Angels of the Shemhamphorash: HAHAHEL (Triune) and MICHAEL (Who is like unto Him)

Day Spirit of the Goetia: #33, GÄAP

> He is a great President and a mighty Prince. He appeareth when the Sun is in some of the southern Signs, in a human shape, going before four great and mighty Kings, as if he were a guide to conduct them along on their way. His office is to make men insensible or ignorant; as also in philosophy to make them knowing, and in all the liberal sciences. He can cause love or hatred, also he can teach thee to consecrate those things that belong to the dominion of Amaymon his King. He can deliver familiars out of the custody of other magicians, and answereth truly and perfectly of things past, present, and to come. He can carry and re-carry men very speedily from one kingdom to another, at the will and pleasure of the Exorcist. He ruleth over 66 Legions of Spirits, and he was of the order of Potentates.

Night Spirit of the Goetia: #69, DECARABIA

> He appeareth in the form of a star in a pentacle, at first; but after, at the command of the Exorcist, he putteth on the image of a man. His office is to discover the virtues of birds and precious stones, and to make the similitude of all kinds of birds to fly before the Exorcist, singing and drinking as natural birds do. He governeth 30 Legions of Spirits, being himself a great Marquis.

Enochian Attributions—from Grand Cross of the Elemental Tablets (see Aces):

			Enochian	*Senior*	*Temple Opening*	*Call*
Air	o	of	hAbioro	Mars	2°=9°	#3
Water	1	of	slgaiol	Venus	3°=8°	#4
Earth	a	of	iCZhihal	King/Sun	1°=10°	#5
	a	of	laidrOM	Mars	1°=10°	#5
	a	of	aCZinoR	Jupiter	1°=10°	#5
	a	of	alhCtGa	Venus	1°=10°	#5
	a	of	ahmlicU	Mercury	1°=10°	#5
Fire	D	of	aapDoce	Venus	4°=7°	#6

EIGHT OF SWORDS
Shortened Force

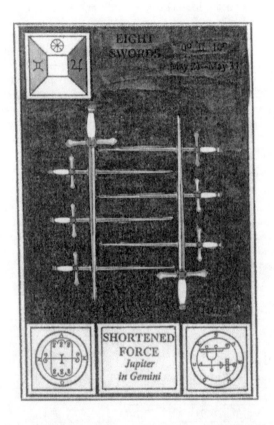

0° to 10° Gemini (May 21 to May 31)

Jupiter in Gemini — Hod of Yetzirah

Color: Red russet.

General divinatory meanings: Interference. Being good-natured at the wrong time. Unexpected bad luck. Energy wasted on unimportant details.

Angels of the Shemhamphorash: UMABEL (Everlasting name over all) and IAHHEL (Supreme essence)

Day Spirit of the Goetia: #7, AMON

> He is a Marquis great in power, and most stern. He appeareth like a wolf with a serpent's tail, vomiting out of his mouth flames of fire; but at the command of the Magician he putteth on the shape of a man with dog's teeth beset in a head like a raven; or else like a man with a raven's head (simply). He telleth all things past and to come. He procureth feuds and reconcileth controversies between friends. He governeth 40 Legions of Spirits.

Night Spirit of the Goetia: #43, SABNOCK (or SAVNOK)

> He is a Marquis, mighty, great and strong, appearing in the form of an armed soldier with a Lion's head, riding on a pale-coloured horse. His office is to build high towers, castles and cities, and to furnish them with armour, etc. Also he can afflict men for many days with wounds and with sores rotten and full of worms. He giveth good familiars at the request of the Exorcist. He commandeth 50 Legions of Spirits.

Enochian Attributions—from Grand Cross of the Elemental Tablets (see Aces):

			Enochian	*Senior*	*Temple Opening*	*Call*
Air	A	of	hTmordA	Moon	$2°=9°$	#3
Water	i	of	ligdisa	Saturn	$3°=8°$	#4
Earth	n	of	lZinopo	Moon	$1°=10°$	#5
Fire	r	of	edLprNaa	King/Sun	$4°=7°$	#6
	r	of	arinnA	Saturn	$4°=7°$	#6

NINE OF SWORDS
Despair and Cruelty

10° to 20° Gemini (June 1 to June 10)

Mars in Gemini — Yesod of Yetzirah

Color: Very dark purple.

General divinatory meanings: Mental anguish. Nothing furthers. Both the acceptance of martyrdom and unrelenting revenge.

Angels of the Shemhamphorash: ANNAUEL (Joyful service) and MEKEKIEL (Vivifying)

Day Spirit of the Goetia: #8, BARBATOS

He is a great Duke, and appeareth when the Sun is in Sagittary, with four noble Kings and their companies of great troops. He giveth understanding of the singing of birds, and the voices of other creatures, such as the barking of dogs. He breaketh the hidden treasures open that have been laid by the enchantments of magicians. He is of the order of Virtues, of which some part he retaineth still; and he knoweth all things past, and to come, and conciliateth friends and those that be in power. He ruleth over 30 Legions of Spirits.

Night Spirit of the Goetia: #44, SHAX (or SHAZ, or SHASS)

He is a great Marquis and appeareth in the form of a stock-dove, speaking with a voice hoarse, but yet subtle. His office is to take away the sight, hearing, or understanding of any man or woman at the command of the Exorcist; and to steal money out of the houses of kings, and to carry it again in 1,200 years. If commanded he will fetch horses at the request of the Exorcist, or any other thing. But he must first be commanded into a triangle Δ, or else he will deceive him, and tell him many lies. He can discover all things that are hidden, and not kept by wicked Spirits.

Enochian Attributions—from Grand Cross of the Elemental Tablets (see Aces):

		Enochian	Senior	Temple Opening	Call
Air	d	of	hTmordA	Moon	2°=9°	#3
Water	s	of	ligdisa	Saturn	3°=8°	#4
Earth	i	of	lZinopo	Moon	1°=10°	#5
Fire	i	of	arinnA	Saturn	4°=7°	#6

TEN OF SWORDS

Ruin

20° to 30° Gemini (June 11 to June 20)

Sol in Gemini — Malkuth of Yetzirah

Colors: Citrine, Olive, Russet, and Black; each flecked gold.

General divinatory meanings: Madness. Disaster which may sig-
nal the end of delusion.

Angels of the Shemhamphorash: DAMABIAH (Fountain of wisdom) and MENIEL (Nourishing all)

Day Spirit of the Goetia: #9, PAIMON

A great King, and very obedient unto Lucifer. He appeareth in the form of a man sitting upon a dromedary with a crown most glorious upon his head. There goeth before him also an host of Spirits, like men with trumpets and well sounding cymbals, and all other sorts of musical instruments. He hath a great voice, and roareth at his first coming, and his speech is such that the Magician cannot well understand unless he can compel him. This Spirit can teach all arts and sciences, and other secret things. He can discover unto thee what the Earth is, and what holdeth it up in the Waters; and what mind is, and where it is; or any other thing thou mayest desire to know. He giveth dignity, and confirmeth the same. He bindeth or maketh any man subject unto the Magician if he so desire it. He giveth good familiars, and such as can teach all arts. He is to be observed towards the West. He is of the order of Dominions. He hath under him 200 Legions of Spirits, and part of them are of the order of Angels, and the other part of Potentates. Now if thou callest this Spirit Paimon alone, thou must make him some offering; and there will attend him two Kings called Labal and Abalim, and also other Spirits who be of the order of Potentates in his host, and 25 Legions. And those Spirits which be subject unto them are not always with them unless the Magician do compel them.

Night Spirit of the Goetia: #45, VINÉ (or VINEA)

He is a great King, and an Earl; and appeareth with the head of a lion, riding upon a black horse, and bearing a viper in his hand. His office is to discover things hidden, witches, wizards, and things present, past, and to come. He, at the command of the Exorcist will build towers, overthrow great stone walls, and make the waters rough with storms. He governeth 36 Legions of Spirits.

Enochian Attributions—from Grand Cross of the Elemental Tablets (see Aces):

			Enochian	Senior	Temple Opening	Call
Air	r	of	hTmordA	Moon	2°=9°	#3
Water	a	of	ligdisa	Saturn	3°=8°	#4
Earth	Z	of	iCZhihal	King/Sun	1°=10°	#5
	Z	of	lZinopo	Moon	1°=10°	#5
Fire	n	of	arinnA	Saturn	4°=7°	#6

TWO OF DISKS

Harmonious Change

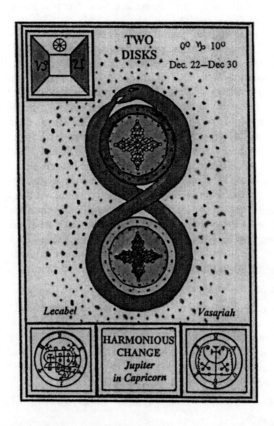

0° to 10° Capricorn (December 22 to December 30)

Jupiter in Capricorn — Chokmah of Assiah

Color: White, flecked red, blue, and yellow.

General divinatory meanings: Change. First manifestation of earth. Perpetual change maintains stability.

Angels of the Shemhamphorash: LECABEL (Teacher) and VASA-RIAH (Upright)

Day Spirit of the Goetia: #28, BERITH (or BEALE or BEAL, or BOFRY, or BOLFRY)

> He is a mighty, great, and terrible Duke. He appeareth in the form of a soldier with red clothing, riding upon a red horse, and having a crown of gold upon his head. He giveth true answers, past, present, and to come. Thou must make use of a ring in calling him forth, as is before spoken of regarding Beleth. He can turn all metals into gold. He can give dignities, and can confirm them unto man. He speaketh with a very clear and subtle voice. He is a great liar, and not to be trusted unto. He governeth 26 Legions of Spirits.

Night Spirit of the Goetia: #64, HAURES (or HAURAS, or HAVRES or FLAUROS)

> He is a great Duke, and appeareth at first like a leopard, mighty, terrible, and strong, but after a while, at the command of the Exorcist, he putteth on human shape with eyes flaming and fiery, and a most terrible countenance. He giveth true answers of all things, present, past, and to come. But if he be not commanded into a triangle, Δ, he will lie in all these things, and deceive and beguile the Exorcist in these things or in such and such business. He will, lastly, talk of the creation of the world, and of divinity, and of how he and other Spirits fell. He destroyeth and burneth up those who be the enemies of the Exorcist should he so desire it; also he will not suffer him to be tempted by any other Spirit or otherwise. He governeth 36 Legions of Spirits.

Enochian Attributions — from Grand Cross of the Elemental Tablets (see Aces):

			Enochian	*Senior*	*Temple Opening*	*Call*
Air	T	of	AVToTar	Mercury	2°=9°	#3
Water	o	of	raagiosl	King/Sun	3°=8°	#4
	o	of	soniznt	Mercury	3°=8°	#4
Earth	R	of	aCZinoR	Jupiter	1°=10°	#5
Fire	e	of	adoeoeT	Jupiter	4°=7°	#6

THREE OF DISKS
Material Works

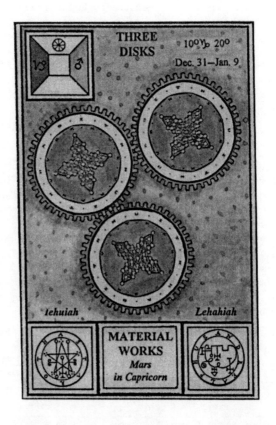

10° to 20° Capricorn (December 31 to January 9)

Mars in Capricorn — Binah of Assiah

Color: Gray-flecked pink.

General divinatory meanings: Constructive energy. Crystallization of forces. Job. Concentrated effort rewarded now or in the future.

Angels of the Shemhamphorash: IEHUIAH (Omniscient) and LEHAHIAH (Merciful)

Day Spirit of the Goetia: #29, ASTAROTH

He is a mighty, and strong Duke, and appeareth in the form of an hurtful angel riding on an infernal beast like a dragon, and carrying in his right hand a viper. Thou must in no wise let him approach too near unto thee, lest he do thee damage by his noisome breath. Wherefore the Magician must hold the magical ring near his face, and that will defend him. He giveth true answers of things past, present, and to come, and can discover all secrets. He will declare wittingly how the spirits fell, if desired, and the reason of his own fall. He can make men wonderfully knowing in all liberal sciences. He ruleth 40 Legions of Spirits.

Night Spirit of the Goetia: #65, ANDREALPHUS

He is a mighty Marquis, appearing at first in the form of a peacock, with great noises. But after a time he putteth on human shape. He can teach geometry perfectly. He maketh men very subtle therein; and in all thing pertaining unto mensuration or astronomy. He can transform a man into the likeness of a bird. He governeth 30 Legions of Infernal Spirits.

Enochian Attributions — from Grand Cross of the Elemental Tablets (see Aces):

	Enochian		Senior	Temple Opening	Call
Air	a	of AVToTar	Mercury	$2°=9°$	#3
Water	n	of soniznt	Mercury	$3°=8°$	#4
Earth	o	of aCZinoR	Jupiter	$1°=10°$	#5
Fire	o	of adoeoeT	Jupiter	$4°=7°$	#6

FOUR OF DISKS

Earthly Power

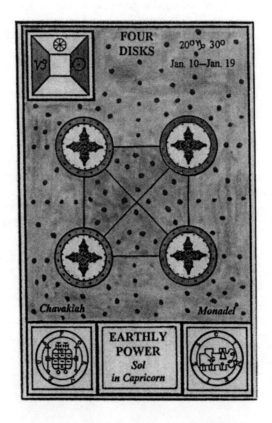

20° to 30° Capricorn (January 10 to January 19)

Sol in Capricorn — Chesed of Assiah

Color: Deep azure-flecked yellow.

General divinatory meanings: Unaggressive mastery over purely material circumstances. Security within protective walls. Law and order.

Angels of the Shemhamphorash: CHAVAKIAH (To be rejoiced in) and MONADEL (Honorable)

Day Spirit of the Goetia: #30, FORNEUS

> He is a mighty and great Marquis, and appeareth in the form of a great sea-monster. He teacheth, and maketh men wonderfully knowing in the art of rhetoric. He causeth men to have a good name, and to have the knowledge and understanding of tongues. He maketh one to be beloved of his Foes as well as of his friends. He governeth 29 Legions of Spirits, partly of the order of Thrones, and partly of that of Angels.

Night Spirit of the Goetia: #66, CIMEIES (or CIMEJES, or KIMARIS)

> He is a Marquis, mighty, great, strong and powerful, appearing like a valiant warrior riding upon a goodly black horse. He ruleth over all Spirits in the parts of Africa. His office is to teach perfectly grammar, logic, rhetoric, and to discover things lost or hidden, and treasures. He governeth 20 Legions of Infernals.

Enochian Attributions — from Grand Cross of the Elemental Tablets (see Aces):

		Enochian	Senior	Temple Opening	Call
Air	r	of AVToTar	Mercury	2°=9°	#3
Water	i	of soniznt	Mercury	3°=8°	#4
Earth	n	of aCZinoR	Jupiter	1°=10°	#5
Fire	d	of edLprNaa	King/Sun	4°=7°	#6
	d	of adoeoeT	Jupiter	4°=7°	#6

FIVE OF DISKS
Material Trouble

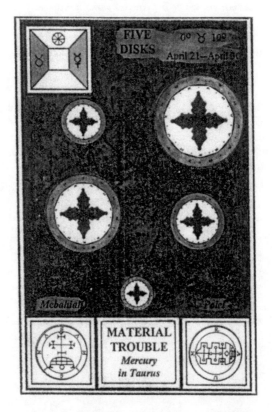

0° to 10° Taurus (April 21 to April 30)

Mercury in Taurus — Geburah of Assiah

Color: Red, flecked black.

General divinatory meanings: Worry. Anxiety over money. Loss of job or source of income. Prolonged inaction produces intense strain. Fundamental instability.

Angels of the Shemhamphorash: MEBAHIAH (Eternal) and POIEL (Supporting all things)

Day Spirit of the Goetia: #4, SAMIGINA (or GAMIGIN)

> He is a great Marquis. He appeareth in the form of a little horse or ass, and then into human shape doth he change himself at the request of the Master. He speaketh with a hoarse voice. He ruleth over 30 Legions of Inferiors. He teaches all liberal sciences, and giveth account of dead souls that died in sin.

Night Spirit of the Goetia: #40, RÄUM

> He is a great Earl; and appeareth at first in the form of a crow, but after the command of the Exorcist he putteth on human shape. His office is to steal treasures out king's houses, and to carry it whither he is commanded, and to destroy cities and dignities of men, and to tell all things, past, and what is, and what will be; and to cause love between friends and foes. He was of the order of Thrones. He governeth 30 Legions of Spirits.

Enochian Attributions—from Grand Cross of the Elemental Tablets (see Aces):

			Enochian	*Senior*	*Temple Opening*	*Call*
Air	z	of	Ahaozpi	Venus	2°=9°	#3
Water	l	of	raagiosl	King/Sun	3°=8°	#4
	l	of	slgaiol	Venus	3°=8°	#4
	l	of	ligdisa	Saturn	3°=8°	#4
	l	of	laoaxrp	Moon	3°=8°	#4
	l	of	lsrahpm	Mars	3°=8°	#4
Earth	M	of	laidrOM	Mars	1°=10°	#5
Fire	t	of	aaetPio	Mars	4°=7°	#6

SIX OF DISKS
Material Success

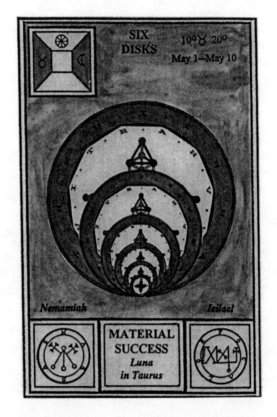

10° to 20° Taurus (May 1 to May 10)

Moon in Taurus — Tiphareth of Assiah

Color: Gold amber.

General divinatory meanings: Investment of labor or resources results in high yields. A settling down. Temporary success.

Angels of the Shemhamphorash: NEMAMIAH (Lovable) and IEILAEL (Hearer of lamentations)

Day Spirit of the Goetia: #5, MARBAS

> He is a great President, and appeareth at first in the form of a great lion, but afterwards, at the request of the Master, he putteth on human shape. He answereth truly of things hidden or secret. He causeth diseases and cureth them. Again, he giveth great wisdom and knowledge in mechanical arts; and can change men into other shapes. He governeth 36 Legions of Spirits.

Night Spirit of the Goetia: #41, FOCALOR (or FORCALORE, or FURCALOR)

> He is mighty Duke and strong. He appeareth in the form of a man with gryphon's wings. His office is to slay men, and to drown them in the waters, and to overthrow ships of war, for he hath power over both winds and seas; but he will not hurt any man or thing if he be commanded to the contrary by the exorcist. He also hath hopes to return to the Seventh Throne after 1,000 years. He governeth 30 Legions of Spirits.

Enochian Attributions—from Grand Cross of the Elemental Tablets (see Aces):

			Enochian	Senior	Temple Opening	Call
Air	p	of	Ahaoz<u>p</u>i	Venus	2°=9°	#3
Water	g	of	raagiosl	King/Sun	3°=8°	#4
	g	of	slgaiol	Venus	3°=8°	#4
Earth	O	of	laidr<u>O</u>M	Mars	1°=10°	#5
Fire	e	of	aa<u>e</u>tPio	Mars	4°=7°	#6

SEVEN OF DISKS
Success Unfulfilled

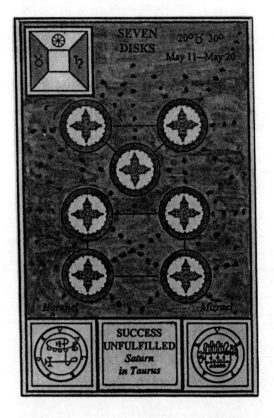

20° to 30° Taurus (May 11 to May 20)

Saturn in Taurus — Netzach of Assiah

Color: Olive, flecked gold.

General divinatory meanings: Expected profits turn into loss or even liabilities.

Angels of the Shemhamphorash: HARAHEL (Permeating all) and MIZRAEL (Raising up the oppressed)

Day Spirit of the Goetia: #6, VALEFOR

He is a mighty Duke, and appeareth in the shape of a lion with an ass's head, bellowing. He is a good familiar, but tempteth them he is a familiar of to steal. He governeth 10 Legions of Spirits.

Night Spirit of the Goetia: #42, VEPAR (or VEPHAR)

He is a Duke great and strong, and appeareth like a mermaid. His office is to govern the waters, and to guide ships laden with arms, armour, and ammunition, etc. thereon. And at the request of the Exorcist he can cause the seas to be right stormy and to appear full of ships. Also he maketh men to die in three days by putrefying wounds or sores, and causing worms to breed in them. He governeth 29 Legions of Spirits.

Enochian Attributions — from Grand Cross of the Elemental Tablets (see Aces):

			Enochian	*Senior*	*Temple Opening*	*Call*
Air	i	of	Ahaozpi	Venus	$2°=9°$	#3
Water	a	of	slgaiol	Venus	$3°=8°$	#4
Earth	r	of	laidrOM	Mars	$1°=10°$	#5
Fire	a	of	edLprNaa	King/Sun	$4°=7°$	#6
	a	of	aapDoce	Venus	$4°=7°$	#6
	a	of	aNodoin	Mercury	$4°=7°$	#6
	a	of	adoeoeT	Jupiter	$4°=7°$	#6
	a	of	aaetPio	Mars	$4°=7°$	#6

EIGHT OF DISKS

Prudence

0° to 10° Virgo (August 23 to September1)

Sol in Virgo — Hod of Assiah

Color: Yellowish brown, flecked white.

General divinatory meanings: "Saving for a rainy day." Plant your garden and wait. Retiring as a positive maneuver.

Angels of the Shemhamphorash: AEHAIAH (Long suffering) and CAHETHEL (Adorable)

Day Spirit of the Goetia: #16, ZEPAR

> He is a great Duke, and appeareth in red apparel and armour, like a soldier. His office is to cause women to love men, and to bring them together in love. He also maketh them barren. He governeth 26 Legions of Inferior Spirits.

Night Spirit of the Goetia: #52, ALLOCES (or ALOCAS)

> He is a Duke, great, mighty, and strong, appearing in the form of a soldier riding upon a great horse. His face is like that of a lion, very red, and having flaming eyes. His speech is hoarse and very big. His office is to teach the art of astronomy, and all the liberal sciences. He bringeth unto thee good familiars; also he ruleth over 36 Legions of Spirits.

Enochian Attributions — from Grand Cross of the Elemental Tablets (see Aces):

			Enochian	Senior	Temple Opening	Call
Air	t	of	hipoṯga	Saturn	$2°=9°$	#3
Water	i	of	raagiosl	King/Sun	$3°=8°$	#4
	i	of	ligdisa	Saturn	$3°=8°$	#4
Earth	o	of	lZinoP̱o	Moon	$1°=10°$	#5
Fire	d	of	aLnḏUod	Moon	$4°=7°$	#6

NINE OF DISKS

Material Gain

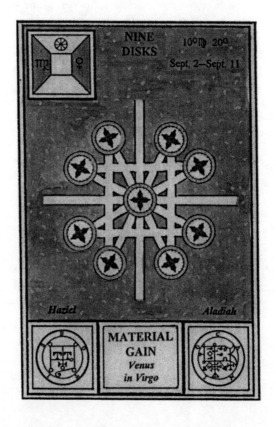

10° to 20° Virgo (September 2 to September 11)

Venus in Virgo — Yesod of Assiah

Color: Citrine, flecked azure.

General divinatory meanings: Considerable increase of fortune. Reap what you've sown and relax. Popularity. Good luck and good management. Inheritance.

Angels of the Shemhamphorash: HAZIEL (Merciful) and ALADIAH (Profitable)

Day Spirit of the Goetia: #17, BOTIS

He is a great President, and an Earl. He appeareth at the first show in the form of an ugly viper, then at the command of the Magician he putteth on a human shape with great teeth, and two horns, carrying a bright and sharp sword in his hand. He telleth all things past, and to come, and reconcileth friends and foes. He ruleth over 60 Legions of Spirits.

Night Spirit of the Goetia: #53, CAMIO (or CAÏM)

He is a great President, and appeareth in the form of the bird called a thrush at first, but afterwards he putteth on the shape of a man carrying in his hand a sharp sword. He seemeth to answer in burning ashes, or in coals of fire. He is a good disputer. His office is to give unto men the understanding of all birds, lowing of bullocks, barking of dogs, and other creatures; and also of the voice of the waters. He giveth true answers to things to come. His was of the order of Angels, but now ruleth over 30 Legions of Spirits Infernal.

Enochian Attributions — from Grand Cross of the Elemental Tablets (see Aces):

			Enochian	*Senior*	*Temple Opening*	*Call*
Air	g	of	hipotga	Saturn	$2°=9°$	#3
Water	g	of	ligdisa	Saturn	$3°=8°$	#4
Earth	P	of	lZinoPo	Moon	$1°=10°$	#5
Fire	n	of	aLndUod	Moon	$4°=7°$	#6

TEN OF DISKS

Wealth

20° to 30° Virgo (September 12 to September 22)

Mercury in Virgo — Malkuth of Assiah

Color: Black rayed with yellow.

General divinatory meanings: Material prosperity. Recycle wealth by acquisitions and philanthropy. If properly applied, true wisdom and perfect happiness.

Angels of the Shemhamphorash: LAUIAH (Meet to be exalted) and HAHIAH (Refuge)

Day Spirit of the Goetia: #18, BATHIN

> He is a mighty and strong Duke, and appeareth like a strong man with the tail of a serpent, sitting upon a pale-colored horse. He knoweth the virtues of herbs and precious stones, and can transport men suddenly from one country to another. He ruleth over 30 Legions of Spirits.

Night Spirit of the Goetia: #54, MURMUR (or MURMUS, or MURMUX)

> He is a great Duke, and Earl; and appeareth in the form of a warrior riding upon a gryphon, with a ducal crown upon his head. There do go before him those his ministers with great trumpets sounding. His office is to teach philosophy perfectly, and to constrain souls deceased to come before the Exorcist to answer those questions which he may wish to put to them, if desired. He was partly of the order of Thrones, and partly of that of Angels. He now ruleth 30 Legions of Spirits.

Enochian Attributions — from Grand Cross of the Elemental Tablets (see Aces):

			Enochian	*Senior*	*Temple Opening*	*Call*
Air	a	of	hipotga	Saturn	2°=9°	#3
Water	d	of	ligdisa	Saturn	3°=8°	#4
Earth	o	of	lZinoPo	Moon	1°=10°	#5
Fire	L	of	edLprNaa	King/Sun	4°=7°	#6
	L	of	aLndUod	Moon	4°=7°	#6

CHAPTER SIX

Tarot Divination

The key to an accurate answer in a tarot reading does not lie in the cards but in the question. Let's say that, as the result of some wonderful cosmic accident, you found yourself in the presence of an all-knowing angel who was willing to give you one accurate and detailed answer to any specific question you might have. What would you ask? Would you ask if there is romance on the horizon? Would you ask which team is going to win the World Series? Would you ask if Lee Harvey Oswald was the lone assassin of President Kennedy? Probably not. If you are like most people you would most likely be paralyzed by indecision, not wishing to waste such a profound gift on a frivolous or mundane question.

Let's assume, though, that after deep thought and meditation, you do arrive at a question that burns at your very soul; a question that distills the mysteries of a thousand other questions; a question that, if answered and understood, would mean both your intellectual enlightenment and your spiritual liberation. You take the question to the angel and you ask it. In response the angel opens the Great Book of Answers, but instead of reading from it, the angel flips through the great book and rips out pages here and there and tosses them at your feet. "The answer at last!" you say to yourself as you gather up the pages from the Great Book of Answers. But upon examination you discover that the various pages are filled with curious pictures, graphs and images which do not make any sense to you. Still, you are confident that the angel has answered truthfully, and you remain steadfast in your conviction that your answer lies in the scattered images. So you sit down and carefully examine every detail of the torn pages, the order in which they were chosen, and their relative position to one another. Finally, after a period of struggle with the demons of ego and wishful thinking, you stop looking for the answer to the question and start examining your real reasons for asking the question in the first place. Is your question prompted by some anxiety you are experiencing? If so, what is the source of that anxiety...a person ...your environment...personal fears...real or imagined shortcomings in your character or personality? Eventually it becomes clear that your question is really a complex weave of interrelated questions, each ready to bare its secrets, but only if you are truly willing to face the truth.

Now the angel's message takes on new dimensions; hidden motives are brought to light, and unrecognized avenues of possibilities appear. From this profoundly wider perspective the meanings of the scattered symbols become quite clear.

The point I am trying to make with the above story probably can be distilled into the following: If you are willing to be painfully honest with yourself when formulating the question, then, in the truest sense, you have already received your answer. Any subsequent observed phenomena—physical, mental, or psychic—can serve as the vehicle of communication of that answer. Tea leaves, pyromancy, coin flipping, bibliomancy, observing the flight of birds, the shape of melted wax when poured into cold water, or anything else can provide the answer if you are truly prepared to receive it. Traditional wisdom, however, suggests that it is easier to perceive the truth within a perfect, or near perfect, medium. The inner workings of the ever-changing universe are mirrored perfectly in the sixty-four hexagrams of the *I Ching*, making it one of the oldest and most revered forms of divination in the world. The Holy Qabalah presents another pure representation of the cosmos in the form of the seventy-eight cards of the tarot.

THE SIGNIFICATOR

Before beginning it is necessary to choose the Significator. The Significator is a card, usually a Court Card, that is used to represent you or the questioner. In the *Tarot of Ceremonial Magick* it can be the Court Card or Small Card that represents the birthday of the questioner.

THE INVOCATION

Prior to any divinatory operation it is important to take a moment to attune yourself and the questioner to the great intelligences with whom you wish to communicate. The adepts of the Golden Dawn created a brief yet effective invocation of these universal agencies which we quote below: Take the cards in your left hand. With the right hand, hold the wand over them (or simply hold the right hand over them) and say:

> *I invoke thee, IAO, that thou wilt send HRU, the great Angel that is set over the operations of this secret Wisdom, to lay his hand invisibly upon these consecrated cards of art, that thereby we may obtain true knowledge of hidden things to the glory of thine ineffable Name. Amen.*

THE SHUFFLE AND CUT

Shuffle the cards thoroughly for one to two minutes, while calmly concentrating on the question. Then set the deck face down upon the table and cut them into two piles (or have the questioner cut them). Place the bottom pile on top.

Turn the entire deck *face up* on the table. Carefully fan the cards out from left to right in a large horseshoe. Without disturbing the order of the cards locate the **Significator.** Being careful to keep the cards in order, take the Significator and all the cards to its right to form a stack. (While this stack is still face up, the Significator should be the bottom card.) Now, again being careful to keep the cards in order, restack the left portion of the horseshoe and place it face up upon the right stack. Now turn the whole deck face down. (The Significator should now be the first card you turn over in the reading.)

There are literally thousands of ways to "read" the tarot cards. The spread we present below is among the simplest to master. The important thing to remember is to be consistent. Once you find a spread that you are comfortable with, stick with it. The efficacy of your readings will only be diluted if you constantly change spreads.

THE CELTIC CROSS SPREAD

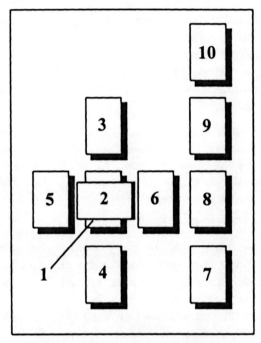

Figure 18. The "Celtic Cross" Spread.

Pick the Significator and lay it face up with no comment. The next card in the deck will be the first card (1) of the reading. Turn it over, lay it upon the Significator and say: "This card covers you and represents the general influences that surround the situation."

Turn over the second card and lay it across the first (position 2 in the diagram), saying: "This card crosses you and shows the opposing forces, whether for good or for ill."

Turn over the third card and place it above the first card, saying: "This crowns you and represents your conscious thoughts in the matter."

Turn over the fourth card and place it below the first card, saying: "This card shows your unconscious thoughts in the matter."

Turn over the fifth card and place it to the left of the first card, saying: "This is behind you and represents the influences that have just passed or that are now passing away."

Turn over the sixth card and place it to the right of the first card, saying: "This is before you and shows the influences that will be operating in the near future."

Turn over the seventh card and place it to the far right of the fourth card (see diagram), saying: "This card represents yourself."

Turn over the eighth card and place it directly above the seventh, saying: "This shows your environment."

Turn over the ninth card and place it directly above the eighth, saying: "This card represents your hopes and fears in the matter."

Turn over the tenth and final card and place it directly above the ninth, saying: "This card tells the final outcome of the matter, the total result of all the influences exerted by the other cards."

It is also very helpful to make general observations:

A majority of Trumps indicates forces beyond the control of the questioner.

A majority of Wands indicates energy, opposition or a quarrel.

A majority of Cups indicates pleasure, merriment or romance.

A majority of Swords indicates trouble, sadness, illness or death.

A majority of Disks indicates business, money, and material possessions.

A majority of Court Cards indicates social gatherings, societies or meetings.

4 Aces indicate great power and force. 3 Aces indicate success and riches.

4 Knights indicate swift moving events. 3 Knights indicate news or unexpected meetings.

4 Queens indicate authority and influence. 3 Queens indicate friends in high places.

4 Princes indicate a meeting with influential and powerful people. 3 Princes indicate rank and position.

4 Princesses indicate new ideas or plans. 3 Princesses indicate youthful gatherings.

4 Tens indicate responsibility and worry. 3 Tens indicate buying and selling.

4 Nines indicate added responsibilities. 3 Nines indicate much correspondence.

4 Eights indicate news. 3 Eights indicate travel.

4 Sevens indicate disappointment. 3 Sevens indicate contracts or treaties.

4 Sixes indicate pleasure. 3 Sixes indicate success and gain.

4 Fives indicate discipline and order. 3 Fives indicate quarreling.

4 Fours indicate peace. 3 Fours indicate industriousness.

4 Threes indicate determination. 3 Threes indicate deceit.

4 Twos indicate conferences or conversations. 3 Twos indicate reorganization or recommencement of a project.

Wands do not mix well with Cups but do with Disks and Swords.

Swords do not mix well with Disks but do with Cups and Wands.

Cups do not mix well with Wands but do with Swords and Disks.

Disks do not mix well with Swords but do with Wands and Cups.

APPENDIX ONE

Astrological Information

COURT CARDS

Figure 19 shows the rulership of the Knights, Queens, and Princes over the Small Cards. The Small Cards each represent ten degrees (one decan) of the zodiac, and the Knights, Queens, and Princes rule from twenty degrees of one sign to twenty degrees of the next.

MOON (CONT.)	EMPEROR			HIEROPHANT			LOVERS		
	QUEEN OF WANDS			PRINCE OF DISKS			KNIGHT OF SWORDS		
10 CUPS	2 WANDS	3 WANDS	4 WANDS	5 DISKS	6 DISKS	7 DISKS	8 SWORDS	9 SWORDS
20 to 30	0 to 10	10 to 20	20 to 30	0 to 10	10 to 20	20 to 30	0 to 10	10 to 20
Pisces	Aries	Aries	Aries	Taurus	Taurus	Taurus	Gemini	Gemini
Mar-11 Mar-20	Mar-21 Mar-30	Mar-31 Apr-10	Apr-11 Apr-20	Apr-21 Apr-30	May-1 May-10	May-11 May-20	May-21 May-31	Jun-1 Jun-10

LOVERS (CONT.)	CHARIOT			LUST			HERMIT		
	QUEEN OF CUPS			PRINCE OF CUPS			KNIGHT OF DISKS		
10 SWORDS	2 CUPS	3 CUPS	4 CUPS	5 WANDS	6 WANDS	7 WANDS	8 DISKS	9 DISKS
20 to 30	0 to 10	10 to 20	20 to 30	0 to 10	10 to 20	20 to 30	0 to 10	10 to 20
Gemini	Cancer	Cancer	Cancer	Leo	Leo	Leo	Virgo	Virgo
Jun-11 Jun-20	Jun-21 Jul-1	Jul-2 Jul-11	Jul-12 Jul-21	Jul-22 Aug-1	Aug-2 Aug-11	Aug-12 Aug-22	Aug-23 Sep-1	Sep-2 Sep-11

HERMIT (CONT.)	JUSTICE			DEATH			ART		
	QUEEN OF SWORDS			PRINCE OF CUPS			KNIGHT OF WANDS		
10 DISKS	2 SWORDS	3 SWORDS	4 SWORDS	5 CUPS	6 CUPS	7 CUPS	8 WANDS	9 WANDS
20 to 30	0 to 10	10 to 20	20 to 30	0 to 10	10 to 20	20 to 30	0 to 10	10 to 20
Virgo	Libra	Libra	Libra	Scorpio	Scorpio	Scorpio	Sagittarius	Sagittarius
Sep-12 Sep-22	Sep-23 Oct-2	Oct-3 Oct-12	Oct-13 Oct-22	Oct-23 Nov-2	Nov-3 Nov-12	Nov-13 Nov-22	Nov-23 Dec-2	Dec-3 Dec-12

ART (CONT.)	DEVIL			STAR			MOON		
	QUEEN OF DISKS			PRINCE OF SWORDS			KNIGHT OF CUPS		
10 WANDS	2 DISKS	3 DISKS	4 SWORDS	5 SWORDS	6 SWORDS	7 SWORDS	8 CUPS	9 CUPS
20 to 30	0 to 10	10 to 20	20 to 30	0 to 10	10 to 20	20 to 30	0 to 10	10 to 20
Sagittarius	Capricorn	Capricorn	Capricorn	Aquarius	Aquarius	Aquarius	Pisces	Pisces
Dec-13 Dec-21	Dec-22 Dec-30	Dec-31 Jan-9	Jan-10 Jan-19	Jan-20 Jan-29	Jan-30 Feb-8	Feb-9 Feb-18	Feb-19 Feb-28	Mar-1 Mar-10

Figure 19. Astrological rulership of the Trumps, Court Cards and Small Cards.

In any given year the days may vary considerably from the table below. When choosing a Significator or when dealing with time periods on or near the cusps of the following degrees and dates please consult an ephemeris or astrological calendar.

Table 1. Zodiacal Significators and Court Cards.

March 11 to April 10	20° Pisces to 20° Aries	Queen of Wands
April 11 to May 10	20° Aries to 20° Taurus	Prince of Disks
May 11 to June 10	20° Taurus to 20° Gemini	Knight of Swords
June 11 to July 11	20° Gemini to 20° Cancer	Queen of Cups
July 12 to Aug. 11	20° Cancer to 20° Leo	Prince of Wands
Aug.12 to Sept. 11	20° Leo to 20° Virgo	Knight of Disks
Sept. 12 to Oct. 12	20° Virgo to 20° Libra	Queen of Swords
Oct. 13 to Nov. 12	20° Libra to 20° Scorpio	Prince of Cups
Nov. 13 to Dec. 12	20° Scorpio to 20° Sagittarius	Knight of Wands
Dec. 13 to Jan. 9	20° Sagittarius to 20° Capricorn	Queen of Disks
Jan. 10 to Feb. 8	20° Capricorn to 20° Aquarius	Prince of Swords
Feb. 9 to March 10	20° Aquarius to 20° Pisces	Knight of Cups

SMALL CARDS

Table 2. Zodiacal Significators and Small Cards.

March 21 to March 30	0° to 10° Aries	2 of Wands
March 31 to April 10	10° to 20° Aries	3 of Wands
April 11 to April 20	20° to 30° Aries	4 of Wands
April 21 to April 30	0° to 10° Taurus	5 of Disks
May 1 to May 10	10° to 20° Taurus	6 of Disks
May 11 to May 20	20° to 30° Taurus	7 of Disks
May 21 to May 31	0° to 10° Gemini	8 of Swords
June 1 to June 10	10° to 20° Gemini	9 of Swords
June 11 to June 20	20° to 30° Gemini	10 of Swords
June 21 to July 1	0° to 10° Cancer	2 of Cups
July 2 to July 11	10° to 20° Cancer	3 of Cups
July 12 to July 21	20° to 30° Cancer	4 of Cups
July 22 to Aug. 1	0° to 10° Leo	5 of Wands
Aug. 2 to Aug. 11	10° to 20° Leo	6 of Wands
Aug. 12 to Aug. 22	20° to 30° Leo	7 of Wands
Aug. 23 to Sept. 1	0° to 10° Virgo	8 of Disks
Sept. 2 to Sept. 11	10° to 20° Virgo	9 of Disks
Sept. 12 to Sept. 22	20° to 30° Virgo	10 of Disks
Sept. 23 to Oct. 2	0° to 10° Libra	2 of Swords
Oct. 3 to Oct. 12	10° to 20° Libra	3 of Swords
Oct. 13 to Oct. 22	20° to 30° Libra	4 of Swords
Oct. 23 to Nov. 1	0° to 10° Scorpio	5 of Cups

Table 2. Zodiacal Significators and Small Cards (cont'd).

Nov. 2 to Nov. 12	10° to 20° Scorpio	6 of Cups
Nov. 13 to Nov. 22	20° to 30° Scorpio	7 of Cups
Nov. 23 to Dec. 2	0° to 10° Sagittarius	8 of Wands
Dec. 3 to Dec. 12	10° to 20° Sagittarius	9 of Wands
Dec. 13 to Dec. 21	20° to 30° Sagittarius	10 of Wands
Dec. 22 to Dec. 30	0° to 10° Capricorn	2 of Disks
Dec. 31 to Jan. 9	10° to 20° Capricorn	3 of Disks
Jan. 10 to Jan. 19	20° to 30° Capricorn	4 of Disks
Jan. 20 to Jan. 29	0° to 10° Aquarius	5 of Swords
Jan. 30 to Feb. 8	10° to 20° Aquarius	6 of Swords
Feb. 9 to Feb. 18	20° to 30° Aquarius	7 of Swords
Feb. 19 to Feb. 28	0° to 10° Pisces	8 of Cups
March 1 to March 10	10° to 20° Pisces	9 of Cups
March 11 to March 20	20° to 30° Pisces	10 of Cups

Rituals of the Pentagram and Hexagram

Prior to any magical operation it is wise to ceremonially banish the working area. This can be as simple or elaborate as the magician sees fit. I have included below a version of the Lesser Banishing Ritual of the Pentagram and encourage anyone intending to do Enochian or Goetic magick never to omit its performance both before *and* after working.

Following the Pentagram Ritual I have also included a version of the Ritual of the Hexagram. The Hexagram operates on the macrocosmic/planetary plane in the same way the Pentagram operates on the microcosmic/elemental plane. If it is your intention to invoke any of the planetary Seniors of the Elemental Tablets, it is necessary to perform the invoking ritual of the Senior's planet by means of the invoking Ritual of the Hexagram. This is done after the Lesser Ritual of the Pentagram, but before the temple opening.

THE LESSER BANISHING RITUAL OF THE PENTAGRAM

(The Qabalistic Cross)[1]
Facing East, touch your forehead and say "**Ateh**" (ah-teh).[2]

---

1. The Qabalistic Cross places the three pillars of the Tree of Life upon the body of the magician. It affirms the magician's identity as a microcosmic representation of the macrocosm, and announces that fact to the magical world.
2. "To Thee."

Touch your heart and say "**Malkuth**" (mal-kooth).[3]

Touch your right shoulder and say "**Ve-Geburah**" (veh-gee-boo-rah).[4]

Touch your left shoulder and say "**Ve-Gedulah**" (veh-gee-doo-lah).[5]

Clasp hands over the heart and say "**Le-Olam** (lee-oh-lam).[6] Amen."

Still facing East, trace in the air with the forefinger of the right hand (or magical wand or dagger) the banishing pentagram of Earth.

Figure 20. Banishing Pentagram of Earth.

Vibrate: "YHVH" (Yod-Hey-Vav-Hey).[7]

Without lowering your arm, turn to the South and trace the banishing pentagram of Earth and vibrate: "ADONAI" (ah-doh-noy).[8]

Without lowering your arm, turn to the West and trace the banishing pentagram of Earth and vibrate: "EHIEH" (eh-hey-yay).[9]

Without lowering your arm, turn to the North and trace the banishing pentagram of Earth and vibrate: "AGLA" (ah-ga-lah).[10]

---

3. "Kingdom."
4. "And Power," alluding to the Pillar of Strength.
5. "And Glory," alluding to the Pillar of Mercy.
6. "To the Ages."
7. See Chapter One.
8. Usually translated "Lord."
9. "I Am."
10. Notariqon of "Ateh Gibor Le-Olahm Adonai"—"Thou art mighty forever my Lord."

Without lowering your arm, return to the East completing the circle.

Stand straight with your arms stretched to the sides, your body forming a cross. Say:

"Before me Raphael (raw-fay-ale).[11]

Behind me Gabriel (gaw-bree-ale).[12]

On my right hand, Michael (mee-ky-ale).[13]

On my left hand, Auriel (oh-ree-ale).[14]

For about me flames the Pentagram, and in the column stands the six-rayed star."

Touch your forehead and say "**Ateh**."

Touch your heart and say "**Malkuth**."

Touch your right shoulder and say "**Ve-Geburah**."

Touch your left shoulder and say "**Ve-Gedulah**."

Clasp hands over the heart and say "**Le-Olam. Amen**."

---

11. Archangel of the East (Air); literally "God has healed."
12. Archangel of the South (Fire); literally "God is my strength."
13. Archangel of the West (Water); literally "Who is as God."
14. Archangel of the North (Earth); literally "Light of God."

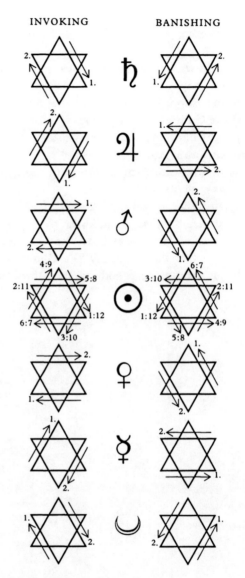

Figure 21. Invoking and Banishing Hexagrams.

THE LESSER RITUAL
OF THE HEXAGRAM

This ritual is to be performed after the Lesser Ritual of the Pentagram.

Stand upright, feet together, left arm at side, right across body, holding Wand or other weapon upright in the median line. Face East and say:

"I.N.R.I.

Yod, Nun, Resh, Yod.

Virgo, Isis, Mighty Mother.

Scorpio, Apophis, Destroyer.

Sol, Osiris, Slain and Risen.

Isis, Apophis, Osiris IAO."

Extend the arms in the form of a cross, and say:

"The Sign of Osiris Slain."

Raise the right arm to point upwards, keeping the elbow square, and lower the left arm to point downwards, keeping the elbow square, while turning the head over the left shoulder looking down so that the eyes follow the left forearm, and say:

"The Sign of the Mourning of Isis."

Raise the arms at an angle of sixty degrees to each other above the head, which is thrown back, and say:

"The Sign of Apophis and Typhon."

Cross the arms on the breast, and bow the head and say:

"The Sign of Osiris Risen."

Give all four signs saying:

"L.V.X., LUX the Light of the Cross."

With the magical weapon trace the appropriate Hexagram in the East, saying, "ARARITA."[15]

Turn to the South and Trace the appropriate Hexagram saying: "ARARITA."

---

15. ARARITA אראריתא. This word consists of the initials of a sentence which means "One is His Beginning: One is His Individuality: His Permutation is One."

Turn to the West and Trace the appropriate Hexagram saying: "ARARITA."

Turn to the North and Trace the appropriate Hexagram saying: "ARARITA."

Return to the East.

Repeat all actions down to "**L.V.X.,** LUX **the Light of the Cross.**"

Temple Openings and Enochian Calls (Elemental)

I encourage the reader before embarking upon Enochian magick, to first outline a simple program of elemental workings; perhaps dedicating several months to the exploration of one Elemental Tablet, or working exclusively with Seniors. Keep detailed notes of all your operations, and try not to be influenced by experiences of other magicians. Enochian magick is not performed by surrendering to the guided imagery of another magician's visions. I am very disappointed at recent attempts to establish an Enochian orthodoxy which presumes to dictate to the reader what he or she should "see" in their visions.

An English translation of the Enochian follows each Call. However, in my opinion, the Calls should be intoned in the Enochian language. It is my firm contention that the spirits who went to the great effort to dictate the Enochian language to Dee and Kelley did not do so just to hear themselves talk, and that the efficacy of the operation hinges upon the vibrations established by the sounds of the Enochian words. It has been my experience that Enochian spirits respond to nearly any effort to pronounce the language. Some of the most remarkable skrying sessions I have ever participated in have followed what I considered to be horribly butchered renditions of the Calls.

The Golden Dawn developed a pronunciation technique whereby the next following Hebrew vowel sound was inserted after every Enochian consonant. *e.g. ah* after *d* (d<u>a</u>leth), *eh* after *b* (b<u>e</u>th), *ey* after *p* (p<u>e</u>). etc. The Calls as they appear in Golden

Dawn material, and in Crowley's classic, "Liber Chanokh,"[1] use this style. While this form of pronunciation is not ineffective, one need only turn to the original Dee material as it appears in *A True & Faithful Relation*,[2] to see that the communicating angels gave no such pronunciation advice; on the contrary, Dee's notes indicate that the words are to be sounded out pretty much as they are written. The versions of the Calls as they appear below are a letter-for-letter translation of the Calls as they were dictated to Dee and Kelley and do not presume to offer any theoretical pronunciation.

After the magician banishes, opens the temple, and intones the appropriate Call or Calls, all that remains is to invoke the individual spirit. To properly do this the names of all the members of the ruling hierarchy must be called out. The lower the spirit is on the hierarchical scale, the more superiors it has.

The temple openings as written below invoke the top of the hierarchy, Three Holy Names of God and the Great Elemental King of the Tablet. After the specific temple opening it is not necessary to repeat these names in the subsequent conjuration.

For a spirit from the Tablet of Union; only the name of the spirit invoked is required in the conjuration.

For a Senior from an Elemental Tablet: only the name of the Senior invoked is required in the conjuration.

For a Kerubic angel from a subangle of an Elemental Tablet: the names of all six Seniors, and the two divine names of the calvary cross of the subangle are all required in the conjuration.

For a Lesser Angel of a subangle of an Elemental Tablet: the names of all six Seniors, the two divine names of the calvary cross

---

1. See *The Enochian World of Aleister Crowley* by Lon Milo DuQuette and Christopher S. Hyatt, Ph.D. (Scottsdale, AZ: New Falcon Publications, 1991), p. 61. See also "Liber Chanokh, A Brief Abstract of the Symbolic Representation of the Universe," Part 2, *The Equinox* I(8) (rpt. York Beach, ME: Samuel Weiser, 1991), p. 99.

2. Meric Casaubon's 1659 publication of Dee's diary notes, *A True and Faithful Relation of what passed for many Yeers between Dr. John Dee ... and some Spirits* (London, 1659; most recent reprint New York: Magickal Childe, 1992).

of the subangle, and the name of the Kerubic angel are all required in the conjuration.

The brief conjuration below has been adapted from Aleister Crowley's Enochian translation of the First Conjuration of the *Goetia.*[3]

Ol vinu   od zacam,   Ils   gah ... [*name of spirit*].
I   invoke and move thee, O thou, Spirit ...   _____

Od   lansh   vors   gi   Iad,
and being exalted above ye in the power of the Most High,

gohus pugo ils,   darbs!
I say   unto thee, obey!

Dooiap   _____, od   _____, od   _____, od   _____ ...
In the name of _____, and _____, and _____, and _____ ...[4]

Ol   vinu   od   zacam,
I do invoke and by invoking conjure thee,

Ils   gah   ... [*name of spirit*].
O thou Spirit ...   _____.

SPIRIT

Ceremony of the Opening of the Portal
of the Vault of the Adepts.
Paroketh, the Veil of the Sanctuary.

(To be used prior to the reading of the First Call)

[*Make the Sign of the Rending of the Veil.*][5]
[*Make the Sign of the Closing of the Veil.*][6]

---

3. Aleister Crowley, ed., *The Goetia*, p. 54.
4. Insert as many names as necessary.
5. Hands together, arms thrust forward; hands then part and draw off to sides, as if parting a veil.
6. Above motion reversed.

[*Make the Invoking Pentagrams of Spirit.*]

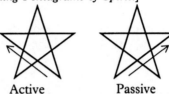

Active   Passive

In the number 21, in the grand word AHIH; In the Name YHShVH, in the Pass Word I.N.R.I., O Spirits of the Tablet of Spirit, Ye, ye I invoke!

The Sign of Osiris Slain! [*make sign*][7]

The Sign of the Mourning of Isis! [*make sign*][7]

The Sign of Apophis and Typhon! [*make sign*][7]

The Sign of Osiris risen! [*make sign*][7]

L.V.X., Lux. The Light of the Cross. [*repeat signs*]

In the name of IHVH ALVH VDOTH. I declare that the Spiritis of Spirit have been duly invoked.

[*Knock 1– 4444.*]

The First Call

(Invokes the entire Tablet of Union)

Ol sonf vors g, gohó Iad Balt, lansh calz vonpho; Sobra zol ror i ta nazpsad, graa ta malprg; Ds holq qaa nothoa zimz, od commah ta nobloh zien; Soba thil gnonp prge aldi; Ds urbs oboleh g rsam; Casarm ohorela caba Pir; Ds zonrensg cab erm iadnah. Philah farzm znurza adna gono Iadpil, ds homtoh; Soba ipam, lu ipamis; Ds loholo vep zomd poamal, od bogpa aai ta piap piomol od vooan. Zacare, ca, od zamran; odo cicle qaa; zorge, lap zirdo noco Mad, hoath Iaida.

I reign over you, saith the God of Justice, in power exalted above the firmaments of wrath; in Whose hands the sun is as a sword, and the moon as a penetrating fire; Who measures your garments in the midst of my vestures, and trussed you together as the

---

7. See Appendix Two, Ritual of the Hexagram.

palms of my hands; Whose seats I garnished with the fire of gathering; Who beautified your garments with admiration; to Whom I made a law to govern the Holy Ones; Who delivered you a rod with the ark of knowledge. Moreover, you lifted up your voices and swore obedience and faith unto Him that lives, and who triumphs; Whose beginning is not, nor end cannot be; Who shines as a flame in the midst of your palace, and reigns amongst you as the balance of righteousness and truth. Move, therefore, and show yourselves; open the mysteries of your creation; be friendly unto me; for I am the servant of the same your God, true worshipper of the Highest.

The Second Call

(Must always be preceded by the First Call)

Invokes the Spirit Column (left-most vertical column EHNB), of the Tablet of Union.

THE FOUR ACES

Adgt upaah zong om faaip sald, viu L? Sobam ialprg izazaz piadph; Casarma abramg ta talho paracleda, q ta lorslq turbs ooge baltoh. Givi chis lusd orri, od micalp chis bia ozongon; lap noan trof cors ta ge, oq manin Iaidon; Torzu, gohe L; zacar, ca, c noqod; zamran micalzo, od ozazm urelp; lap zir Ioiad.

Can the wings of the winds understand your voices of wonder, o you the second of the First? Whom the burning flames have framed within the depth of my jaws: Whom I have prepared as cups for a wedding, or as the flowers in their beauty for the chamber of righteousness. Stronger are your feet than the barren stone, and mightier are your voices than the mainifold winds; for you are become a building such as is not, but in the mind of the All-Powerful. Arise, says the First; move, therefore, unto his servants; show yourselves in power, and make me a strong seer of things; for I am of Him that lives forever.

AIR

The Opening of the Temple in the Grade of 2°=9°

[*Give the Sign of Shu.*[8] *Knock.*]

Let us adore the Lord and King of Air! Shaddai El Chai! Almighty and ever-living One, be Thy Name ever magnified in the Life of All. [*Give Sign of Shu.*] Amen!

[*Make the Invoking Pentagram of Spirit Active.*]

Say: AHIH AGLA EXARP

[*Make the Invoking Pentagram of Air.*]

Say: IHVH ShDI AL ChI

And Elohim said: Let us make Adam in Our own image, after our likeness, and let them have dominion over the fowls of the air. In the Names of IHVH and of ShDI AL ChI, Spirits of Air, adore your Creator! [*With the dagger make the symbol of Aquarius.*] In the name of Raphael and in the Sign of Man, Spirits of Air, adore your Creator! [*Make a cross over the Tablet or Card.*] In the Names and Letters of the Great Eastern Quadrangle, Spirits of Air, adore your Creator! [*Hold the dagger aloft.*] In the Three Great Secret Names of God, ORO IBAH AOZPI that are borne upon the Banners of the East, Spirits of Air, adore your Creator! [*Again raise the*

---

8. The Sign of 2°=9°, the God Shu supporting the sky. Stand erect, upper arms lifted to the sides level with shoulders; forearms up forming right angles to upper arms and shoulders; hands flat, palms up as if supporting a great weight.

dagger.] In the Name of **BATAVIAH**, Great King of the East, Spirits of Air, adore your Creator! In the Name of Shaddai Al Chai. I declare that the Spirits of Air have been duly invoked.

[*Knock: 333–333–333.*]

The Third Call

(Invokes **EXARP** line of the Tablet of Union; the entire Air Tablet; and the Air Subangle of the Air Tablet)

PRINCE OF SWORDS

Micma, goho Piad, zir comselh a zien biah os londoh. Norz chis othil gigipah, undl chis ta puim, q mospleh teloch, quiin toltorg chisi chis ge, m ozien, ds t brgda od torzul. I li eol balzarg, od aala thiln os netaab, dluga vomsarg lonsa capmiali vors cla, homil cocasb, fafen izizop od miinoag de g netaab, vaun nanaeel, panpir malpirgi caosg pild. Noan unalah balt od vooan. Dooiap Mad, goholor, gohus, amiran. Micma iehusoz cacacom, od dooain noar micaolz aai om; Casarmg gohia: Zacar, uniglag, od imvamar pugo plapli ananael qaan.

Behold, says your God, I am a circle on whose hands stand twelve kingdoms. Six are the seats of living breath, the rest are as sharp sickles, or the horns of death, wherein the creatures of the earth are and are not, except by my own hands, which also sleep and shall rise. In the first I made you stewards, and placed you in seats twelve of government, giving unto every one of you power successively over 456, the true ages of time, to the intent that, from the highest vessels and the corners of your governments, you might work my power, pouring down the fires of life and increase on the earth continually. Thus you are become the skirts of justice and truth. In the name of the same, your God, lift up, I say, yourselves. Behold His mercies flourish, and His Name is become mighty amongst us; in Whom we say: Move, descend, and apply yourselves unto us, as unto the partakers of the secret wisdom of your Creation.

WATER

The Opening of the Temple in the Grade of 3°=8°

[*Give the Sign of Auramoth.*]⁹

Let us adore the Lord and King of Water! Elohim Tzabaoth! Elohim of Hosts! Glory be to the Ruach Elohim which moved upon the Face of the Waters of Creation! [*Give Sign of Auramoth.*] Amen!

[*Make the Invoking Pentagram of Spirit Passive.*]

Say: AHIH AGLA HCOMA

[*Make the Invoking Pentagram of Water.*]

Say: AL ALHIM TzBAVTh

And Elohim said: Let us make Adam in Our image; and let them have dominion over the Fish of the Sea! In the Name of Al, Strong and Powerful, and in the name of ALIM TzBAVTh, Spirits of Water, adore your Creator! [*Make symbol of the Eagle with cup.*] In the name of Gabriel and in the sign of the Eagle, Spirits of Water, adore your Creator! [*Make a cross with the cup over the Tablet or Card.*] In all the Names and Letters of the Great Western Quadrangle, Spirits of Water, adore your Creator! [*Elevate the cup.*] In the Three Great Secret Names of God MPH ARSL GAIOL that are borne upon the Banners of the West, Spirits of Water, adore your Creator! [*Raise cup again.*] In the Name of RAAGIOSL,

---

9. The Sign of 3°=8°. Stand erect, upper arms lifted to the sides level with the shoulders, forearms pointing down over the chest; thumbs and fingers of hands form a water triangle (apex pointing down) over the center of the chest.

Great King of the West, Spirits of Water, adore your Creator! In the Name of Elohim Tzabaoth, I declare that the Spirits of Water have been duly invoked.

[*Knock: 1–333–1–333.*]

The Fourth Call

(Invokes HCOMA line of the Tablet of Union; the entire Water Tablet; and the Water Subangle of the Water Tablet)

QUEEN OF CUPS

Othil lasdi babage, od dorpha, gohol: g chis ge avavago cormp pd, ds sonf viu diu? Casarmi oali mapm, sobam ag cormpo crp l, casarmg croodzi chis od ugeg; ds t, capimali, chis capimaon; od lonshin chis ta lo cla. Torgu, nor quasahi, od f caosga; bagle zir enay Iad, ds i od apila. Dooaip Qaal, zacar, od zamran obelisong, rest el aaf nor molap.

I have set my feet in the south, and have looked about me, saying: are not the thunders of increase numbered 33, which reign in the second angle? Under whom I have placed 9639, whom none has yet numbered but one, in whom the second beginning of things are and wax strong; which also successively, are the number of time; and their powers are as the first 456. Arise, you sons of pleasure, and visit the earth for I am the Lord your God, which is and lives. In the name of the Creator, move, and show yourselves as pleasant deliverers, that you may praise him amongst the sons of men.

EARTH

The Opening of the Temple in the Grade of $1° = 10°$

[*Give the Sign of the God SET fighting.*][10]

---

10. The Sign of $1°=10°$. Stand erect, right foot slightly forward; right arm and hand raised forward at an angle of 60° (much like the Roman military salute); left arm and hand at side and pointed down and slightly back.

[*Purify with Fire and Water, and announce:*] The Temple is cleansed.

[*Knock.*] Let us adore the Lord and King of Earth! Adonai ha Aretz, Adonai Melekh, unto Thee be the Kindom, the Sceptre, and the Splendour: Malkuth, Geburah, Gedulah, The Rose of Sharon and the Lily of the Valley, Amen! [*Sprinkle Salt before the Earth Tablet.*] Let the Earth adore Adonai!

[*Make the Invoking Hexagram of Saturn.*]

[*Make the Invoking Pentagram of Spirit Passive.*]

Say: **AHIH AGLA NANTA**

[*Make the Invoking Pentagram of Earth.*]

Say: **ADNI MLK**

"And Elohim said: Let us make Adam in Our image; and let them have dominion over the Fish of the Sea and over the Fowl of the Air: and over every creeping thing that creepeth upon the Earth. And the Elohim created ATh-hADAM: in the image of the Elohim created They them; male and female created They them. In the NAME OF ADNI MLK, and of the Bride and Queen of the Kingdom; Spirits of Earth adore your Creator. [*Make Symbol of the Taurus.*] In the name of Aurial, great archangel of Earth, Spirits of Earth, adore your Creator! [*Make a cross with the cup over the Tablet or Card.*] In the Names and Letters of the Great Northern Quadrangle, Spirits of Earth, adore your Creator! [*Sprinkle water before Earth Tablet.*] In the Three Great Secret Names of God, MOR, DIAL, HCTGA, that are borne upon the Banners of the North, Spirits of Earth, adore your Creator! [Cense the Tablet.] In the name of ICZHIHAL, Great King of the North, Spirits of Earth, adore your Creator! In the Name of Adonai Ha-Aretz, I declare that the Spirits of Earth have been duly invoked.

[*Knock: 4444–333–22–1.*]

The Fifth Call

(Invokes NANTA line of the Tablet of Union; the entire Earth Tablet; and the Earth Subangle of the Earth Tablet)

PRINCESS OF DISKS

Sapah zimii d diu, od noas ta quanis Adroch, dorphal caosg, od faonts piripsol ta blior; casarm amipzi naz arth af, od dlugar zizop zlida caosgi tol torgi; od z chis esiasch l ta viu, od iaod thild, ds hubar peoal, soba cormfa chis ta la, uls od q cocasb. Ca niis od darbs qaas; f etharzi od bliora; iaial ednas cicles, bagle ge Iad L.

The mighty sounds have entered in the third angle, and are become as olives on the Mount of Olives, looking with gladness upon the earth, and dwelling in the brightness of the heavens as comforters; unto whom I fastened pillars of gladness nineteen, and gave them vessels to water the earth with her creatures; and they are the brothers of the first and second, and the beginning of their own seats, which are garnished with continual burning lamps 69636, whose numbers are as the first, the ends and the content of time. Therefore come and obey your creation; visit us in peace and comfort; include us as receivers of your mysteries, because our Lord and Master is all One.

FIRE

The Opening of the Temple in the Grade of $4° = 7°$

[*Give the Sign of Thoum-aesh-neith.*][11]

---

11. The Sign of $4°=7°$. Stand erect, upper arms lifted to the sides level with shoulders; forearms pointing up over the face; thumbs and fingers of haands form a fire triangle (apex pointing up) over the center of the forehead.

[*Knock.*] Let us adore the Lord and King of Fire! Tetragramm-aton Tzabaoth! Blessed be Thou! The Leader of Armies is Thy Name!

[*Make the Invoking Pentagram of Spirit Active.*]

Say: AHIH AGLA BITOM.

[*Make the Invoking Pentagram of Fire.*]

Say: ALHIM IHVH TzBAVTh.

[*Make the Symbol of Leo with censer or Wand.*]

In the name of Michael, archangel of Fire, Spirits of Fire, adore your Creator!" [*Make a cross with the cup over the Tablet or Card.*] In the Names and Letters of the Great Southern Quadrangle, Spirits of Fire, adore your Creator! [*Elevate censer or Wand.*] In the Three Great Secret Names of God, OIP, TEAA, PDOCE, that are borne upon the Banners of the South, Spirits of Fire, adore your Creator! [*Lower and elevate censer or Wand.*] In the name of EDLPRNAA, Great King of the South, Spirits of Fire, adore your Creator! In the Name of IHVH TzBAVTh, I declare that the Spirits of Fire have been duly invoked.

[*Knock: 333–1–333.*]

The Sixth Call

(Invokes BITOM line of the Tablet of Union; the entire Fire Tablet; and the Fire Subangle of the Fire Tablet)

KNIGHT OF WANDS

Gah s diu em, micalzo pilzin; sobam el harg mir babalon od obloc samvelg, dlugar malprg ar caosgi, od acam canal; sobol zar f bliard caosgi, od chis a netab od miam ta viu od d. Darsar solpeth bien; brita od zacam g micalzo sobha ath trian luiahe od ecrin Mad qaaon.

The spirits of the fourth angle are nine, mighty in the firmament of waters; whom the first has planted as a torment to the wicked and a garland to the righteous, giving unto them fiery darts to winnow the earth, and 7699 continual workmen; whose courses visit with comfort the earth, and are in government and continuance as the second and third. Wherefore harken unto my voice; I have talked of you, and I move you in power and presence, you whose works shall be a song of honor and the praise of your God in your creation.

The Seventh Call

(Invokes "A" Square of EXARP of the Tablet of Union; the Water Subangle of the Air Tablet)

QUEEN OF SWORDS

Raas i salman paradiz, oecrimi aao ialpirgah, quiin Enay butmon, od i noas ni paradial, casarmg ugear chirlan; od zonac luciftian, cors ta vaul zirn tol hami; soba londoh od miam chis ta d od es, umadea od pi bliar, othil rit od miam. C noquol rit, zacar, zamran, oecrimi Qadah; od omicaolz aai om; bagle papnor i dlugam lonshi, od umplif ugegi bigliad.

The east is a house of virgins, singing praises amongst the flames of first glory, wherein the Lord has opened his mouth, and they are become 28 living dwellings, in whom the strength of man rejoices; and they are appareled with ornaments of brightness, such as work wonders on all creatures; whose kingdoms and continuance are as the third and fourth, strong towers and places of comfort, the seats of mercy and continuance. O you servants of mercy, move, appear, sing praises unto the Creator; and be mighty amongst us; for to this remembrance is given power, and our strength waxes strong in our comforter.

The Eighth Call

(Invokes "R" Square of EXARP of the Tablet of Union;
the Earth Subangle of the Air Tablet)

PRINCESS OF SWORDS

Bazm, elo, i ta piripson oln naz avabh ox, casarmg uran chis ugeg; ds abramig baltoha, goho Iad; solamian trian ta lolcis abai vovin, od aziagiar rior. Irgil chis da ds paaox busd caosgo, ds chis, od ip uran teloah cacrg oi salman lonhco, od vovina carbaf! Niiso, bagle avavago gohon; niiso, bagle mamao siaion, od mabza Iado i, as, momar, poilp. Niis, zamran ciaofi caosgo, od bliors, od cors i ta abramig.

The midday, the first, is as the third heaven made of pillars of hyacinth 26, in whom the elders are become strong; which I have prepared for my own righteousness, says the Lord; whose long continuance shall be as bucklers to the stooping dragon, and like unto the harvest of a widow. How many are there which remain in the glory of the earth, which are, and shall not see death until this house fall, and the dragon sink! Come away, for the thunders have spoken; come away, for the crowns of the temple, and the coat of Him that is, was, and shall be crowned, are divided. Come, appear to the terror of the earth, and to our comfort, and of such as are prepared.

The Ninth Call

(Invokes "P" Square of EXARP of the Tablet of Union;
the Fire Subangle of the Air Tablet)

KNIGHT OF SWORDS

Micaolz bransg prgel, napta ialpor (ds brin efafafe p vonpho olani od obza, sobca upaah chis tatan, od tranan balye) alar lusda sobol, od chis holq c noquodi cial. Unal aldon mom caosgo ta las ollor gnay limlal. Amma chiis sobca madrid z chis! Ooanoan chis aviny drilpi caosgin, od butmoni parm zumvi cnila: daziz ethamz a childao, od mirc ozol chi pidiai collal. Ulcinin a sobam ucim, bagle Iad Baltoh chirlan par. Niiso (od ip ofafafe)! Bagle a cocasb i cors ca unig blior.

A mighty guard of fire, with two-edged swords flaming (which have vials eight of wrath for two times and a half, whose wings are of wormwood, and of the marrow of salt), have settled their feet in the west, and were measured with their ministers 9996. These gather up the moss of the earth as the rich man does his treasure. Cursed are they whose iniquities they are! In their eyes are millstones greater than the earth, and from their mouths rain seas of blood: their heads are covered with diamonds, and upon their hands are marble sleeves. Happy is he on whom they frown not, because the God of Righteousness rejoices in them. Come away (and not your vials) ! For the time is such as requires comfort.

The Tenth Call

(Invokes "C" Square of HCOMA of the Tablet of Union;
the Air Subangle of the Water Tablet)

PRINCE OF CUPS

Coraxo chis cormp od blans lucal aziazior paeb, soba lilonon chis virq op eophan od raclir maasi bagle caosgi, ds ialpon dosig od basgim, od oxex dazis siatris, od salbrox cynxir faboan. Unal chis const ds daox cocasg ol oanio yor vohim ol gizyax, od eors cocasg plosi molvi, ds page ip, larag om droln matorb cocasb. Emna l patralx yolci matb, nomig monons olora gnay angelard. Ohio Ohio Ohio Ohio Ohio Ohio, noib, Ohio caosgon, bagle madrid i, zirop, chiso drilpa. Niiso—crip ip nidali.

The thunders of judgment and wrath are numbered and are harbored in the north in the likeness of an oak, whose branches are nests 22 of lamentation and weeping laid up for the earth, which burn night and day, and vomit out the heads of scorpions, and live sulphur mingled with poison. These are the thunders that 5678 times in the 24th part of a moment roar with a hundred mighty earthquakes, and a thousand times as many surges, which rest not, not know any echoing time. Here one rock brings forth a thousand, even as the heart of man does his thoughts. Woe, Woe Woe Woe Woe Woe, yes, Woe be to the earth, for her iniquity is, was, and shall be great. Come away—but not your noises.

The Eleventh Call

(Invokes "M" Square of HCOMA of the Tablet of Union;
the Earth Subangle of the Water Tablet)

PRINCESS OF CUPS

Oxiayal holdo od zirom o coraxo ds zildar raasy, od vabzir camliax
od bahal: Nisso! salman teloch! casarman holq, od t i ta z chis soba
cormf i ga. Niisa! Bagle abramg noncp. Zocare, ca, od zamran; odo
cicle qaa; zorge, lap zirdo noco Mad, hoath Iaida.

The mighty seat groaned and there were five thunders which
flew into the east, and the Eagle spake and cried with aloud: Come
away! from the house of death! And they gathered themselves
together and became (those) of whom it is measured, and it is as
they are whose number is 31. Come away! For I prepare for you.
Move, therefore, and show yourselves; open the mysteries of you
creation; be friendly unto me, for I am the servant of the same God
as you, the true worshipper of the Highest.

The Twelfth Call

(Invokes "A" Square of HCOMA of the Tablet of Union;
the Fire Subangle of the Water Tablet)

KNIGHT OF CUPS

Nonci ds sonf babage, od chis ob, hubaio tibibp allar atraah, od ef!
Drix fafen mian, ar Enay ovof, Soba dooain aai i Vonph. Zacar,
gohus, od zamran; odo cicle qaa; zorge lap zirdo noco Mad, hoath
Iaida.

O you that reign in the south, and are 28, the lanterns of sorrow
bind up your girdles, and visit us! Bring down your followers 3663,
that the Lord may be magnified, Whose name amongst you is
Wrath. Move, I say, and show yourselves; open the mysteries of
your creation; be friendly unto me, for I am the servant of the same
God as you, the true worshipper of the Highest.

The Thirteenth Call

(Invokes first "A" Square of NANTA of the Tablet of Union;
the Air Subangle of the Earth Tablet)

PRINCE OF DISKS

Napeai babagen, ds brin vx ooaona lring vonph doalim, eolis ollog
orsba ds chis affa; micma isro Mad, od lonshi Tox, ds i umd aai
grosb; zacar od zamran; odo cicle qaa; zorge, lap zirdo noco Mad,
hoath Iaida.

O you swords of the south, which have 42 eyes to stir up the
wrath of sin, making men drunken which are empty; behold the
promise of God, and the power of Him, which is called amongst
you a bitter sting; move and show yourselves; open the mysteries
of your creation; be friendly unto me, for I am the servant of the
same God as you, the true worshipper of the Highest.

The Fourteenth Call

(Invokes second "N" Square of NANTA of the Tablet of Union;
the Water Subangle of the Earth Tablet)

QUEEN OF DISKS

Noromi bagie, pasbs Oiad, ds trint mirc ol thil, dods tol ham caosgo
homin; ds brin oroch quar; micma bial Oiad, a isro Tox, ds i um
aai Baltim; zacar od zamran; odo cicle qaa; zorge, lap zirdo noco
Mad, hoath Iaida.

O you sons of fury, the daughters of the Just, which sit upon 24
seats, vexing all creatures of the earth with age; which have under
you 1636; behold the voice of God, the promise of Him, which is
called amongst you extreme justice; move and show yourselves;
open the mysteries of your creation; be friendly unto me, for I am
the servant of the same God as you, the true worshipper of the
Highest.

The Fifteenth Call

(Invokes second "A" Square of NANTA of the Tablet of Union;
the Fire Subangle of the Earth Tablet)

KNIGHT OF DISKS

Ils tabaan l ialprt, casarman upaahi chis darg, ds oado caosgi orscor, ds omax monasci Baeovib od emetgis iaiadix: zacar od zamran; odo cicle qaa; zorge, lap zirdo noco Mad, hoath Iaida.

O thou the governor of the first flame, under whose wings are 6379, which weave the earth with dryness, who knowest the great name Righteousness and the seal of honor: move and show yourselves; open the mysteries of your creation; be friendly unto me, for I am the servant of the same God as you, the true worshipper of the Highest.

The Sixteenth Call

(Invokes "I" Square of BITOM of the Tablet of Union; the Air Subangle of the Fire Tablet)

PRINCE OF WANDS

Ils viu ialprt salman balt, ds acroodzi busd, od bliorax balit; ds insi caosg lusdan emod ds om od tliob: drilpa geh ils Mad Zilodarp. Zacar od zamran; odo cicle qaa; zorge, lap zirdo noco Mad, hoath Iaida.

O thou second flame, the house of justice, who hast thy beginning in glory, and shall comfort the just; who walkest on the earth with feet 8763 that understand and separate creatures: great art thou in the God of Stretch-forth-and-Conquer. Move and show yourselves; open the mysteries of your creation; be friendly unto me, for I am the servant of the same God as you, the true worshipper of the Highest.

The Seventeenth Call

(Invokes "T" Square of BITOM of the Tablet of Union; the Water Subangle of the Fire Tablet)

QUEEN OF WANDS

Ils d ialprt, soba upaah chis nanba zixlay dodsih, od brint taxs hubaro tustax ylsi, soba Iad i vonpo unph: aldon dax il od toatar. Zacar od zamran; odo cicle qaa; zorge, lap zirdo noco Mad, hoath Iaida.

O thou third flame, whose wings are thorns to stir up vexation, and who hast 7336 living lamps going before thee, whose God is wrath in anger: gird up the loins of thee and harken. Move and show yourselves; open the mysteries of your creation; be friendly unto me, for I am the servant of the same God as you, the true worshipper of the Highest.

The Eighteenth Call

(Invokes "O" Square of BITOM of the Tablet of Union; the Earth Subangle of the Fire Tablet)

PRINCESS OF WANDS

Ils micaolz olpirt ialprg bliors, ds odo busdir Oiad ovoars caosgo; casarmg laiad eran brints cafafam; ds i umd a q loadohi Moz, od maoffas: bolp como bliort pambt. Zacar od zamran; odo cicle qaa; zorge, lap zirdo noco Mad, hoath Iaida.

O thou mighty light and burning flame of comfort, which openest the glory of God to the centre of the earth; in whom the secrets of truth 6332 have their abiding; which is called in thy kingdom Joy, and not to be measured: be thou a window of comfort unto me. Move and show yourselves; open the mysteries of your creation; be friendly unto me, for I am the servant of the same God as you, the true worshipper of the Highest.

ENOCHIAN CALLS
(THE THIRTY ÆTHYRS)

The thirty Æthyrs are explored one at a time starting with 30, TEX. The Nineteenth Call is used for each of them. The only variation between Calls is the insertion of the name of the Æthyr in the first sentence of the Call.

There is no temple opening indicated for magical workings of the thirty Æthyrs. At the very least I suggest the performance of the Lesser Banishing Ritual of the Pentagram before and after the skrying session.

Each Æthyr is inhabited by three[12] Governors who personify their environment and serve as guides and counselors. After intoning the Call, vibrate the name of each Governor one at a time. Test any beings who appear in your vision with the names of the governors. If they appear to grow stronger or clearer when you repeat the name, then it is likely you have your Governor. If, on the other hand, they appear frightened or repelled by the name, then it is likely that another entity has strayed into your vision and must be ordered out. Do not be frightened if any of the visions or entities at first appear somewhat terrifying. Maintain an attitude of dispassionate curiosity and always keep your cool.

There will come a juncture in your Æthyric workings where you will cease to receive a vision of the Æthyr. This most likely will be because you have reached a point beyond your initiatory level. In this case, you may look for the key to your spiritual advancement in the last Æthyr you could successfully access. Obviously this could be a lifetime (or longer) endeavor. The important thing is to keep a truthful record of all your experiences so you can periodically review and reevaluate your magical progress.

The Nineteenth Call

THE CALL OF THE THIRTY ÆTHYRS

Madriax ds praf (name of Aethyr), chis micaolz saanir caosgo, od fifis balzizras Iaida! Nonca gohulim: Micma adoian Mad, iaod bliorb, Soba ooana chis luciftias peripsol; Ds abraasa noncf netaaib caosgi, od tilb adphaht damploz, tooat noncf g micalz oma, lrasd tofglo marb yarry Idoigo; od torzulp iaodaf, gohol: caosga, tabaord saanir, od christeos yrpoil tiobl, busdir tilb noaln paid orsba od dodrmni zylna. Elzap tilb, parm gi peripsax, od ta qurlst booapis. L nibm, oucho symp; od christeos ag toltorn mirc q tiobl lel. Ton paombd, dilzmo aspian; od christeos ag l tortorn parach a symp. Cordziz, dodpal od fifalz l smnad; od fargt, bams omaoas. Conisbra od avavox, tonug. Orsca tbl, noasmi tabges levithmong; unchi omp

---

12. Except the 30th Æthyr, TEX, which has four Governors.

tilb ors. Bagle? Moooah ol cordziz. L capimao ixomaxip, od ca
cocasb gosaa; baglen pi tianta a babalond, od faorgt teloc vovim.
Madriiax torzu! Oadriax orocha, aboapri. Tabaori priaz ar tabas;
adrpan cors ta dobix; yolcam priazi ar coazior, od quasb qting.
Ripir paaoxt saga cor; uml od prdzar, cacrg aoiveae cormpt. Torzu,
zacar, od zamran aspt sibsi butmona, ds surzas Tia baltan; od cicle
qaa, od ozazma plapli iadnamad.

O you heavens which dwell in the (name of Æthyr), which are
mighty in the parts of the earth, and which execute the judgment
of the Highest! To you it is said: Behold the face of your God, the
beginning of comfort, Whose eyes are the brightness of heavens;
Who provided you for the government of the earth, and her
unspeakable variety, furnishing you with a power of understanding,
to dispose all things according to the providences of Him that sits
on the Holy Throne; and Who rose up in the beginning, saying: the
earth, let her be governed by her parts, and let there be division in
her, that the glory of her may be always drunken and vexed in itself.
The course of her, let it run with the heavens, and as a handmaid
let her serve them. One season, let it confound another; and let
there be no creature upon or within her the same. All her members,
let them differ in their qualities; and let there be no one creature
equal with another. The reasonable creatures of the earth, let them
vex and week out one another; and the dwelling places, let them
forget their names. The works of man and his pomp, let them be
defaced. The buildings of her, let them become caves for the beasts
of the field; confound the understanding of her with darkness.
Why? I regret that I made man. One while let her be known, and
another while a stranger; because she is the bed of an harlot, and
the dwelling place of him-that-is-fallen. O you heavens, arise! The
lower heavens underneath you, let them serve you. Govern those
that govern; cast down such as fall; bring forth with those that
increase, and destroy the rotten. No place let it remain in one number; add and diminish, until the stars be numbered. Arise, move,
and appear before the covenant of His mouth, which He has sworn
unto us in His justice; open the mysteries of your creation, and
make us partakers of undefiled knowledge.

Table 3. Governors of the Thirty Æthyrs.

	AETHYR NAME	GOVERNORS
1.	LIL	OCCODON, PASCOMB, VALGARS
2.	ARN	DOAGNIS, PACASNA, DIALIVA
3.	ZOM	SAMAPHA, VIROOLI, ANDISPI
4.	PAZ	THOTANP, AXZIARG, POTHNIR
5.	LIT	LAZDIXI, NOCAMAL, TIARPAX
6.	MAZ	SAXTOMP, VAVAAMP, ZIRZIRD
7.	DEO	OPMACAS, GENADOL, ASPIAON
8.	ZID	ZAMFRES, TODNAON, PRISTAC
9.	ZIP	ODDIORG, CRALPIR, DOANZIN
10.	ZAX	LEXARPH, COMANAN, TABITOM[13]
11.	ICH	MOLPAND, VANARDA, PONODOL
12.	LOE	TAPAMAL, GEDOONS, AMBRIOL
13.	ZIM	GECAOND, LAPARIN, DOCEPAX
14.	VTA	TEDOOND, VIUIPOS, OOANAMB
15.	OXO	TAHANDO, NOCIABI, TASTOXO

13. The names LEXARPH, COMANAN, and TABITOM are taken from "The Black Cross," a double version of the Tablet of Union that separates the four Elemental Tablets in much the same way as the Grand Crosses separate the subangles of each Tablet. The names of the remaining eighty-eight Governors are taken from the Elemental Tablets themselves.

Table 3. Governors of the Thirty Æthyrs (cont'd).

	AETHYR NAME	GOVERNORS
16.	LEA	CUCARPT, LANACON, SOCHIAL
17.	TAN	SIGMORF, AYDROPT, TOCARZI
18.	ZEN	NABAOMI, ZAFASAI, YALPAMB
19.	POP	TORZOXI, ABAIOND, OMAGRAP
20.	KHR	ZILDRON, PARZIBA, TOTOCAN
21.	ASP	CHIRSPA, TOANTOM, VIXPALG
22.	LIN	OZIDAIA, PARAOAN, CALZIRG
23.	TOR	RONOAMB, ONIZIMP, ZAXANIN
24.	NIA	ORANCIR, CHIALPS, SOAGEEL
25.	VTI	MIRZIND, OBUAORS, RANGLAM
26.	DES	POPHAND, NIGRANA, BAZCHIM
27.	ZAA	SAZIAMI, MATHULA, ORPAMB
28.	BAG	LABNIXP, FOCISNI, OXLOPAR
29.	RII	VASTRIM, ODRAXTI, GOMZIAM
30.	TEX	TAONGLA, GEMNIMB, ADVORPT, DOZINAL

Figure 22. Enochian Tablet of Union (English).

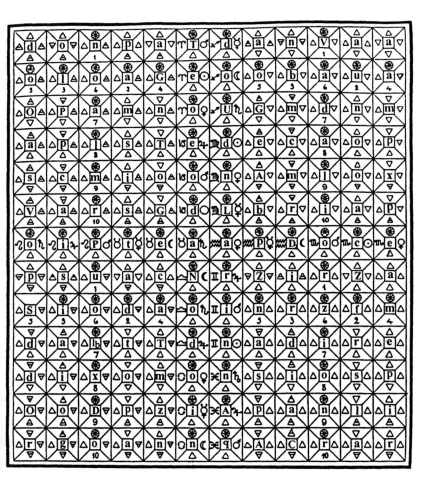

Figure 23. Enochian Elemental Fire Tablet (English).

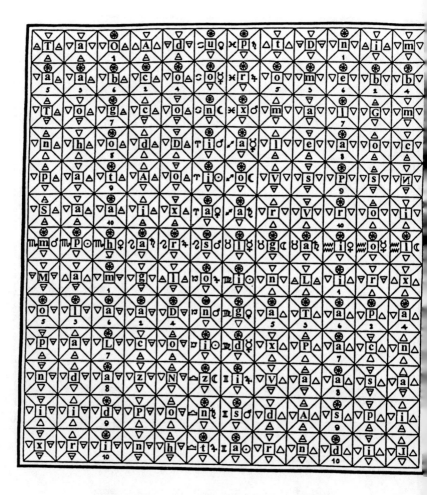

Figure 24. Enochian Elemental Water Tablet (English).

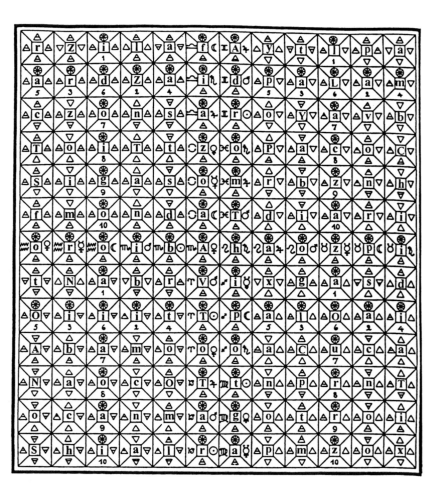

Figure 25. Enochian Elemental Air Tablet (English).

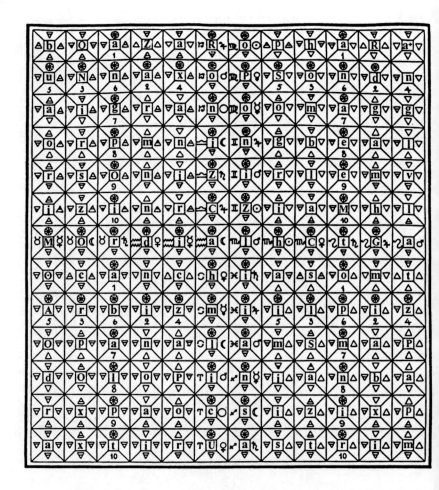

Figure 26. Enochian Elemental Earth Tablet (English).

APPENDIX FOUR

Goetic Evocation

The trappings of Goetic evocation resemble a Christopher Lee Gothic horror film. The magician stands inside a magical circle, protected by the names of God, archangels, angels, and other qabalistic words of power. By a combination of powerful (yet eloquent) exorcisms, and terrifyingly incomprehensible barbarous words of evocation, the magician calls forth a demon from the pits of hell and traps it in a magical triangle. There it reluctantly waits to hear its master's instructions. Then, as is usually the case in horror films, the magician, because of some tragic character flaw (or unresolved issue stemming from his childhood in a dysfunctional family) loses his grip on the demon and is plunged to hell after being killed in a most unspeakably grotesque (yet poetically fitting) manner.

While it is true that Goetic evocations are sometimes accompanied by strange, sometimes unexplainable phenomena, in nearly twenty years of practice I have yet to encounter anything resembling the above colorful scenario. I do recognize, to the filmmaker's credit, the basic elements of this form of magick. Yes! the magician stands inside a magical circle upon which are divine names. Yes! the spirit is called forth by conjurations and strange words, and is trapped in a triangle. Yes! the spirit is of the infernal variety and (at least in the mind of the magician) can be very dangerous if not carefully controlled.

The obvious question becomes at this point; why on earth would anyone in their right mind[1] involve themselves in such an

---

1. To many critics, a magician in his or her "right mind" is any oxymoron.

enterprise? For those who have not been irreparably damaged by simplistic and paranoid religious programing, the answer lies in the understanding of the term "infernal spirit."

How many of us can truthfully say that we have never allowed greed, or jealousy, or insecurity, or lust, or laziness to ruin a potential triumph? How many times have you said to yourself, "I am my own worst enemy"? Couldn't these bad habits and character flaws be viewed as nasty little imps who pop up at the worst possible times and torpedo even the best laid plans? Wouldn't we just love to master them and force them to work for our benefit instead of our undoing?

Certainly, from one perspective, "hell"[2] is our own psyche, and the infernal spirits can be considered portions of the unconscious mind, or aspects of our emotional life. Up until the moment of evocation these "demons" remain uncontrolled and undirected. The various spirits of classical magical literature are convenient (and some say uncannily accurate) personifications of these various potential powers. What makes them dangerous is the fact that unless they are called forth and forced to labor in harmony with the magician's will, they will continue to run amok and work their mischief.

The seventy-two spirits of the Goetia are drawn from one of the best known grimiores of all time, the *Lesser Key of Solomon*, the first book of the *Lemegeton*.[3] Several of the spirits appear to be degenerated versions of the gods of the ancients, *e.g.*, Bael, Astaroth (Astarte) and Belial; while others appear to be the genii of the *Alf Laylah wa Laylah* (*A Thousand and One Nights*, or *The Arabian Nights*).

---

2. Middle English "helle," Anglo-Saxon "hel," meaning hidden, concealed.

3. Sloane manuscript nos. 2731 and 3648, currently housed in the British Library. These papers are dated 1697 and appear to be one collector's attempt to have his favorite texts of Solomonic magick bound in a single volume. They bear evidence that their language has been modernized, and that they were transcribed from far older volumes, how old we do not know.

Those who in the past translated, copied and recopied the various texts of the *Lemegeton* were obviously not sympathetic to the pagan theology represented by the spirits, and so we can never be sure what the original attributes of the spirits actually were. The mere fact that they have come down to us as "fallen angels" of the classic Miltonian ilk, is suspect in itself. Even more striking is the sex negative attitude displayed by the fact that all the spirits are male, including the Dukes Ashtaroth (the Goddess Astarte), and Gremory (who appears as a beautiful woman) and Vepar (a Mermaid).

There are those, whose opinions I respect very much, who maintain that the spirits of the *Goetia* have an objective existence and can and do operate independently of the magician's will. There are others who aver that they are entirely subjective and have no existence outside of the magician's mind. Aleister Crowley went so far in his introduction to the *Goetia*[4] to say that its spirits are portions of the human brain which, if properly isolated and disciplined, can be of great aid to the magician. But elsewhere in his writings it appears he takes an entirely different attitude.

Whatever the true nature of the spirits may be, it is obvious to anyone who has been bold (or reckless) enough to perform a Goetic evocation that things happen. It seems obvious that part of what makes the magick of evocation work is the magician's acceptance (at least temporally) that the spirit's existence is objective.

Goetic magicians fall into two broad categories; those who strive as far as humanly possible to replicate what they believe to be the original *modus operandi,* and those who don't. Neither, in my opinion, is necessarily superior to the other. It all depends upon the individual magician. If your religious conviction or sense of art is such that you feel that the evocation is doomed to failure if you do not have every word of every conjuration, constraint, or curse, duly memorized exactly as it appears in the 1687 Sloane

---

4. See *The Book of the Goetia of Solomon the King* (Inverness, Scotland: Society for the Propagation of Religious Truth, 1904). Reprinted (New York: Magickal Childe Publishing, 1989).

manuscript; if you believe that you will be blasted, torn apart, and have your soul eaten by a hideous halitosis-snorting monster if one Hebrew word upon your magical circle is misspelled, then it is absolutely essential that you take the time to meticulously do all these things correctly.

On the other hand, if you feel confident that there is a simple formula of attitude and action that is the key to a successful evocation, and that as long the basic elements of that formula are mastered the operation will be a success, then it would be a waste of time to memorize conjurations that are meaningless to you, or guard your circle with the names of gods you do not worship. It is probably clear to the reader that I fall into the latter category.

Space prohibits me to adequately elucidate much further upon either traditional or "heretical" Goetia. The best I can do is offer a brief outline of the system and refer you to two texts that I feel best represent the two schools of thought. First the books: *The Goetia*,[5] and *Aleister Crowley's Illustrated Goetia* by Lon Milo DuQuette and Christopher S. Hyatt, Ph.D.[6] The former is a faithful reproduction of the first book of the *Lemegeton* which was transcribed by S. L. MacGregor Mathers and introduced by Aleister Crowley. This text contains all of the various conjurations and constraints, plus the seals and attributes of the spirits, and many details relevant to a classic evocation. Anyone who seriously wants to embark up Goetic evocation must be profoundly familiar with this text. The latter is an attempt by Dr. Hyatt and myself to point out the psychological treasures in Goetic evocation and give examples of modern innovations in the system. We have included selected classical conjurations and, of course, the seals and attributes of all the spirits. This text also includes seventy-two illustrations by artist and Goetic magician, David P. Wilson. Even if I were not co-author of this text I would recommend it to any student of Goetia.

---

5. See note 4.
6. Scottsdale: New Falcon Publications, 1992.

ELEMENTS OF GOETIC EVOCATION

The circle and triangle are the two most important physical elements of a Goetic evocation and are considered indispensable. (See figures 27 and 28 on pp. 263 and 264.) The operator stands in the center of the circle, representative of the infinite universe and the magician's own aura. It is a place of balance and stability. The circle is protected by the divine names sacred to the magician. For the duration of the ceremony, the magician never steps outside of the circle. The spirit is called forth into a triangle placed about three feet east of the circle.[7] The base of the triangle is positioned toward the circle. The triangle is framed by three names considered holy to the magician. A copy of the spirit's seal is placed inside the triangle, and another copy of the seal, with the Pentagram (see figure 29, p. 265) inscribed upon the reverse side, is worn as a medallion around the neck of the magician. Upon the spirit's arrival, both sides of the medallion are displayed to the spirit to force it to obedience. The magician should also have a version of the Hexagram of Solomon (see figure 30, p. 265) pinned or otherwise displayed somewhere upon his or her robe.

The magician must feel absolutely confident in his or her justification and ability to call up the spirit. In the classic text, the magician spends a great deal of time praising the greatness of God and itemizing all the miracles wrought by him through the holy personages of the past. ("You did it for Moses, you did it for Elijah! Won't you please do it for me?") This shameless brownnosing was very necessary to the medieval magician whose psyche was imprinted with a literal belief in biblical events (not to

---

7. A modern technique of Goetic evocation, made popular by C. (Poke) Runyon and N. White, utilizes a black mirror or speculum in the triangle. The magician is positioned so that he or she can see his or her own face reflected in the speculum. When the spirit appears it is through the distorted image of the magician's own face. Another Runyon technique has two people in the circle; an operator, who recites the conjuration and directs the evocation; and a receiver who holds a candle in each hand and stands in front of the operator. The receiver alone gazes into the speculum and receives the vision.

mention heaven and hell). The modern magician must achieve the same exalted feeling of divine justification in his or her conjuration. The method will vary between individuals but the result must be an unambiguous feeling of self-righteous justification.

After this attitude is achieved, the next phase is to induce a subjective state of mind so that communication with the spirit does not seem to be an absurd, irrational occurrence. This has been done traditionally by the recitation of the barbarous words of evocation. Continuous babbling of these strange sounding words serves to excite the magician's imagination and refocus the mind to a sphere where communication with a demon is not an unthinkable activity. I have included at the end of this appendix a version of the Preliminary Invocation[8] of the *Goetia* that contains the classic barbarous words of evocation. For years my only conjuration was this invocation. In Aleister Crowley's personal copy of the *Goetia* he had transcribed the First Enochian call (see Appendix 3), leading some scholars to speculated that in his later years, Crowley discovered that Enochian calls could be used for Goetic evocations. I have found that the recitation of the First and Second Enochian Calls, in place of more traditional conjurations and the "barbarous words of evocation," is indeed a most efficacious conjuration.

It has been suggested that the proper state of mind can be attained through the ingestion of psychoactive substances. I hasten to caution the reader that, even though I believe it is possible to access the magical plane by the use of drugs, it is difficult, if not impossible, to properly execute the remaining necessary components of the ritual. In other words, you may be able to evoke the spirit while high, but then may discover that it is difficult to remember what exactly you wanted to do with it. This is a very dangerous place to be.

Once you feel exalted and justified, and have put yourself in the receptive state of mind, nothing remains but to call the spirit.

---

8. Invocation calls a spirit or deity into yourself. Evocation calls forth a spirit outside of one's self.

No matter what technique is used, the power that accomplishes this is your pure will.

Even though the original texts contain a series of progressively stronger conjurations and constraints which are to be used if the spirit is reluctant to appear, it is my belief that if you are properly exalted and justified, the spirit will come without additional conjurations or curses. If you have a second or third or fourth conjuration ready because you are not confident that your first conjuration will work, you will most likely need them all.

If, on the other hand, a spirit has promised to do something for you and fails, you are obliged to threaten it in a subsequent evocation. The ultimate threat is to destroy the spirit by burning its seal. This represents total annihilation of the spirit. To give the spirit a taste of this punishment, it is a traditional custom to put the seal in a small metal box (sometimes perforated with holes) with a small amount of sulfur[9] at the bottom. A chain should be attached to two sides of the box. Being careful not to step outside of the circle, the magician uses the blade of the magical sword to suspend the box over a fire (kindled for this purpose and placed within the triangle) while he or she reminds the spirit of its obligation. If, after this act of ceremonial intimidation, the spirit still has not obeyed to your satisfaction, make good on your threat and destroy its seal.[10] Do not attempt to call that particular spirit ever again. It is truly a case of "if you are not for me, you are against me." You can live without it.

You may or may not actually "see" the spirit. You may only sense its presence. Once you know it is in the triangle, give it its orders (charge) and demand that it agrees to comply. Be very precise in your wording of the charge and make sure there are no loopholes in your demands. Be polite but do not dawdle or engage

---

9. No sulfur? Goetic magician James Kababick tells us burning rubber bands makes a perfectly terrible smell.

10. A copy of the seal, hand-drawn on paper or parchment, is adequate. It should not be necessary for you to destroy an actual *Tarot of Ceremonial Magick* card (unless, of course, you promise me you will buy a whole new deck).

in any negotiations or arguments. You are the boss. The spirit should be told that if your wishes are met, you will be a kind master. You may state that if you are happy with its performance you will engrave its seal in precious metal or otherwise immortalize its memory. Tell it that its spiritual status will be elevated as yours is elevated.[11] Do not fall for any suggestions from the spirit to give it offerings, sacrifices, or pacts. That is another kind of magic.

Once you have given the spirit its charge and received assurance that it will be done, then immediately give it licence to depart, being careful to remind it that you want everything accomplished without any harm being done to you, your family, your friends, your pets, your possessions, etc.

The following is a summary outline of a Goetic evocation. But please avail yourself of the above-mentioned texts before attempting the ceremony.

Before beginning a Goetic evocation ask yourself the following questions:

Do I have a very good reason to raise the spirit?

Do I feel absolutely justified and competent to perform the operation?

Do I have a sufficient emotional tie to the object of the operation? (If there is no such emotional link, the evocation will most likely fail. The desire to evoke the spirit must reach the emotional strata of the magician's psyche, for that is the abode of the Goetic spirits.)

Is it my unambiguous will to succeed in the operation?

Do I have the courage to plumb the depths of hell to achieve my ends?

Be brutally truthful with yourself. If there are any doubts as to your answers to any of the questions, cancel the ceremony or

---

11. See "Final Thoughts on Goetic Evocation" toward the end of this appendix.

postpone it until such time as there are none. If you are resolute in your will to proceed, then do the following:

1. In a clean, uncluttered room, draw, tape, or otherwise make a circle approximately nine feet in diameter. Upon the circle write the divine names sacred to your personal form of spiritual discipline.

2. About three feet east of the circle, draw, tape, or otherwise make a triangle, each side measuring two and one half to three feet. Upon the three sides write words of power sacred to your personal form of spiritual discipline.

3. Inside the triangle draw a circle. Within this circle place an incense burner, incense, and a parchment or paper copy of the seal of the spirit you wish to evoke.

4. Prior to the ceremony bathe with the full intention of cleansing the body in preparation for this serious work. Put on a clean magical robe reflective of your highest initiatory degree. This robe should also bear the image of a Hexagram (to identify with the macrocosm).

5. Arm yourself with the wand, and wear the medallion displaying the spirit's seal on one side and the pentagram (to show mastery of the microcosm) on the other. Prior to entering the circle purify the temple with water, and consecrate it with fire. This can be done as elaborately or as simply as your sense of art demands.

6. Entering the circle first perform the Lesser Banishing Ritual of the Pentagram (see Appendix Two).

7. Recite the Preliminary Invocation of the *Goetia*, or the First and Second Enochian Call, or the conjuration or conjurations of your choice.

8. Greet the spirit courteously upon its arrival.

9. Politely give it a specific, well thought out charge, and demand a positive answer.

10. Politely give it license to depart being careful to stipulate that it carry out its orders without harm to you or your loved ones.

11. Banish the temple with the Lesser Banishing Ritual of the Pentagram and wait until such time as you cannot feel any residual of the spirit's presence.

12. Snap out of it. Do whatever it takes to return to everyday objective consciousness. If you still feet "spooky" and "magical," banish again.
13. Break down the temple.
14. Failure of the spirit to perform as promised requires that you evoke the spirit again and issue a threat. Failing again, re-evoke and torment the spirit in the fire box. Failing again, re-evoke for the purpose of destroying the seal completely.
15. While the experience is fresh in your mind, sit down and write a detailed record of the operation.

FINAL THOUGHTS
ON GOETIC EVOCATION

For many the above procedure may seem a childish excursion into role-playing ... an adult Dungeons & Dragons. But isn't day-to-day life a role-playing game? Perhaps we should simply view Goetic evocation as a formal, conscious dialog and relationship between the conscious mind (the magician) and a portion of the unconscious mind (the spirit). The will of the magician to control the spirit is focused by the physical and mental preparations of the ceremony of evocation, and the spirit appears (either objectively or subjectively) upon the seal in the triangle. This "vision" alone serves to charge the seal by indelibly imprinting the magician's unconscious mind with that image. Years from now the magician may forget that he or she ever performed that particular evocation, but the unconscious mind will not forget. Once a spirit has been evoked, a permanent relationship is formed which can only be severed if the magician chooses to "update" his or her unconscious mind with another imprinted image. This can be done ceremonially with the same care and preparation expended in the original evocation.

A Goetic spirit, once evoked, is an awakened giant ready to serve you. You do not want to forget there is an awakened giant in the cellar. This is why one should never forget where he or she has put an activated seal. Traditionally such items are stored in elaborately decorated or otherwise luxurious boxes or bags. Each time the magician's eyes fall upon the container he or she is reminded of the evocation, of the spirit, of how the spirit is pledged to the magician's service. This conscious reinforcement of the relationship serves to recharge both the magician and the spirit. Every time you see or think about the seal housed in its special container you should feel the same warmth of satisfaction as a dog's master feels when he or she is able to feed their loyal pet a special treat.

How do you share your good fortune and spiritual success with a spirit? This question can only be answered by each magician. I am reminded of the old American cowboy movies where the hero rescues the girl and captures the bank robbers, but only after he has been pulled out of a deadly pool of quicksand by his faithful wonder-horse. In the really old movies the cowboy doesn't kiss the girl at the end of the film—he kisses his horse! In other words, give credit where credit is due. You must recognize that your evolution is linked to the spirit's evolution. This recognition can be private and entirely internalized.

In my particular magical/spiritual discipline I seek union with a divine counterpart which is called in Western Hermeticism the Holy Guardian Angel. By no stretch of the imagination have I yet to achieve complete communion with this "being," but I have been vouchsafed glimpses in moments of ecstatic wonder when I realize, however briefly, that I am part of an unimaginably profound greater life. Using my metaphoric vocabulary, these moments are my Holy Guardian Angel attempting to "raise me up."

To a Goetic spirit, you are like the Holy Guardian Angel. Just as there are people in the world who are so base and ignorant that they will end this incarnation without ever being moved by a spiritual impulse, so too are there Goetic spirits who may not be ready to be calmed down enough to have a relationship with you. Only you will know the details of your relationship with the spirits and only you will know how to share your good fortune and spiritual success.

PRELIMINARY INVOCATION
OF THE GOETIA

Thee I invoke, the Bornless one.

Thee, that didst create the Earth and the Heavens:

Thee, that didst create the Night and the Day.

Thee, that didst create the Darkness and the Light.

Thou art Osorronophris: Whom no man hath seen at any time.

Thou art Iabas:

Thou art Iapos:

Thou hast distinguished between the Just and the Unjust.

Thou didst make the Female and Male.

Thou didst produce the Seed and the Fruit.

Thou didst form Men to love one another, and to hate one another.

I am Mosheh (or your name or motto) Thy Prophet, unto Whom Thou didst commit Thy Mysteries, the Ceremonies of Ishrael (or your spiritual discipline):

Thou didst produce the moist and the dry, and that which nourisheth all created Life.

Hear Thou Me, for I am the Angel of Paphro Osorronophris: this is Thy True Name, handed down to the Prophets of Ishrael (or your spiritual discipline).

Air

[*In the East.*]

Hear Me:

Ar: Thiao: Rheibet: Atheleberseth: A Blatha; Abeu: Ebeu: Phi: Thitasoe: Ib: Thiao.

Hear Me, and make all Spirits subject unto Me: so that every Spirit of the firmament and of the Ether: upon the Earth and under the Earth: on dry Land and in the Water: of Whirling Air, and of rushing Fire: and every Spell and Scourge of God may be obedient unto Me.

Fire

[In the South.]

I invoke Thee, the Terrible and Invisible God: Who dwellest in the Void Place of the Spirit:

Arogogorobrao: Sothou: Modorio: Phalarthao: Ooo: Ape, The Bornless One:

Hear Me, and make all Spirits subject unto Me: so that every Spirit of the firmament and of the Ether: upon the Earth and under the Earth: on dry Land and in the Water: of Whirling Air, and of rushing Fire: and every Spell and Scourge of God may be obedient unto Me.

Water

[In the West.]

Hear Me:

Roubriao: Mariodam: Balbnabaoth: Assalonai: Aphniao: I Thoteth: Abrasar: Aeoou: Ischure, Mighty and Bornless One!

Hear Me, and make all Spirits subject unto Me: so that every Spirit of the firmament and of the Ether: upon the Earth and under the Earth: on dry Land and in the Water: of Whirling Air, and of rushing Fire: and every Spell and Scourge of God may be obedient unto Me.

Earth

[In the North.]

I invoke Thee:

Ma: Barraio: Ioel: Kotha: Athorebalo: Abraoth:

Hear Me, and make all Spirits subject unto Me: so that every Spirit of the firmament and of the Ether: upon the Earth and under the Earth: on dry Land and in the Water: of Whirling Air, and of rushing Fire: and every Spell and Scourge of God may be obedient unto Me.

Spirit

[Finish in the East and return to center of Circle.]

Hear me!

Aoth: Abaoth: Basum: Isak: Sabaoth: Iao:

This is the Lord of the Gods:

This is the Lord of the Universe:

This is he Whom the Winds fear.

This is he, who having made Voice by his Commandment, is Lord of All Things; King, Ruler and Helper.

Hear Me, and make all Spirits subject unto Me: so that every Spirit of the firmament and of the Ether: upon the Earth and under the Earth: on dry Land and in the Water: of Whirling Air, and of rushing Fire: and every Spell and Scourge of God may be obedient unto Me.

Hear Me:

Ieou: Pur: Iou: Pur: Iaot: Iaeo: Ioou: Abrasar: Sabriam: Oo: Uu: Adonaie: Ede: Edu: Angelos ton Theon: Aniala Lai: Gaia: Ape: Diathanna Thorun.

I am He! the Bornless Spirit! having sight in the feet: Strong, and the Immortal Fire!

I am He! the Truth!

I am He! Who hate that evil should be wrought in the World!

I am He! that lighteneth and thundereth.

I am He, from whom is the Shower of the Life of Earth:

I am He, the Begetter and Manifester unto the Light:

I am He, the Grace of the World:

"The Heart Girt with Serpent" is My Name!

Come Thou forth, and follow Me: and make all Spirits subject unto Me so that every Spirit of the firmament, and of the Ether: upon the Earth and under the Earth: on dry land, or in the Water: of whirling Air or of rushing fire: and every Spell and Scourge of God, may be obedient unto me!

Iao: Sabao:

Such are the Words!

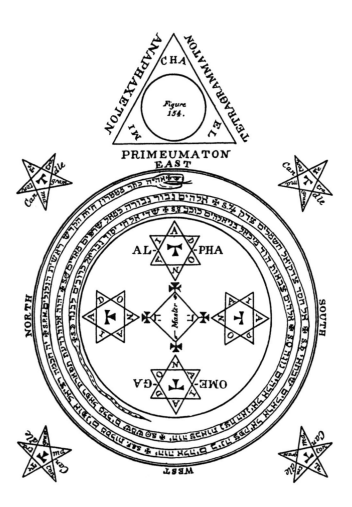

Figure 27. Traditional magical circle and triangle.

Figure 28. Modern example of a magical circle and triangle.

Figure 29. Pentagram of Solomon.

Figure 30. Hexagram of Solomon.

Liber Arcanorum τῶν *Atu* τοῦ *Tahuti quas vidit Asar in Amennti Sub Figura CCXXXI Liber Carcerorum* τῶν *Qliphoth cum suis Geniis. Adduntur Sigilla et Nomina Eorum*

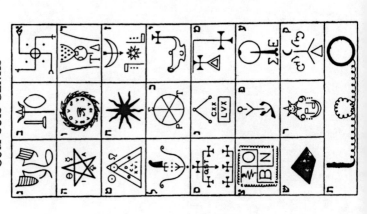

LIBER XXII DOMARUM MERCURII CUM SUIS GENIIS

LIBER XXII CARCERORUM QLIPHOTH CUM SUIS GENIIS

0. A, the heart of IAO, dwelleth in ecstasy in the secret place of the thunders. Between Asar and Asi he abideth in joy.
1. The lightnings increased and the Lord Tahuti stood forth. The Voice came from the Silence. Then the One ran and returned.
2. Now hath Nuit veiled herself, that she may open the gate of her sister.
3. The Virgin of God is enthroned upon an oyster-shell; she is like a pearl, and seeketh Seventy to her Four. In her heart is Hadit the invisible glory.
4. Now riseth Ra-Hoor-Khuit, and dominion is established in the Star of the Flame.
5. Also is the Star of the Flame exalted, bringing benediction to the universe.
6. Here then beneath the winged Eros is youth, delighting in the one and the other.
7. He is Asar between Asi and Nepthi; he cometh forth from the veil.

    He rideth upon the chariot of eternity; the white and the black are harnessed to his car Therefore he reflecteth the Fool, and the sevenfold veil is reveiled.
8. Also came forth mother Earth with her lion, even Sekhet, the lady of Asi.
9. Also the Priest veiled himself, lest his glory be profaned, lest his word be lost in the multitude.

10. Now then the Father of all issued as a mighty wheel; the Sphinx, and the dog-headed god, and Typhon, were bound on his circumference.

11. Also the lady Maat with her feather and her sword abode to judge the righteous.

    For Fate was already established.

12. Then the holy one appeared in the great water of the North; as a golden dawn did he appear, bringing bene-diction to the fallen universe.

13. Also Asar was hidden in Amennti; and the Lords of Time swept over him with the sickle of death.

14. And a mighty angel appeared as a woman, pouring vials of woe upon the flames, lighting the pure stream with her brand of cursing. And the iniquity was very great.

15. Then the Lord Khem arose, He who is holy among the highest, and set up his crowned staff for to redeem the universe.

16. He smote the towers of wailing; he brake them in pieces in the fire of his anger, so that he alone did escape from the ruin thereof.

17. Transformed, the holy virgin appeared as a fluidic fire, making her beauty into a thunderbolt.

18. By her spells she invoked the Scarab, the Lord Kheph-Ra, so that the waters were cloven and the illusion of the towers was destroyed.

19. Then the sun did appear unclouded, and the mouth of Asi was on the mouth of Asar.

20. Then also the Pyramid was builded so that the Initiation might be complete.

21. And in the heart of the Sphinx danced the Lord Adonai, in His garlands of roses and pearls making glad the concourse of things; yea, making glad the concourse of things.

THE GENII OF THE 22 SCALES OF THE SERPENT
AND OF THE QLIPHOTH

א Aₑu-iao-uₑa[ₑ = y]	Amprodias
ב Beₑθaoooabitom	Baratchial
ג Gitωnosapφωllois	Gargophias
ד Dηnaᵹartarωθ [ᵹ = st]	Dagdagiel
ה Hoo-oorω-iᵹ	Hemethterith
ו Vuaretza—[a secret name follows]	Uriens
ז Zooωasar	Zamradiel
ח Chiva-abrahadabra-cadaxviii	Characith
ט Θalₑᵹer-ā-dekerval	Temphioth
י Iehuvahaᵹanₑθatan	Yamatu
כ Kerugunaviel	Kurgasiax
ל Lusanaherandraton	Lafcursiax
מ Malai	Malkunofat
נ Nadimraphoroiozₑθalai	Niantiel
ס Salaθlala-amrodnaθₑiᵹ	Saksaksalim
ע Oaoaaaoooₑ-iᵹ	A'ano'nin
פ Puraθmetai-apηmetai	Parfaxitas
צ Xanθaᵹeranₑϙϙ-iᵹ [ϙϙ =sh, q] . . .	Tzuflifu
ק QaniΔnayx-ipamai	Qulielfi
ר Ra-a-gioselahladnaimawa-iᵹ	Raflifu
ש Shabnax-odobor	Shalicu
ת Thath'th'thithₑthuth-thiᵹ	Thantifaxath

Bibliography

Case, Paul Foster. *The Tarot, A Key to the Wisdom of the Ages.* Los Angeles: Builders of the Adytum, 1990.

———. *The Book of Tokens, Tarot Meditations.* Los Angeles: Builders of the Adytum, 1972.

Cassaubon, Meric. *A True and Faithful Relation of What Passed For Many Years Between Dr. John Dee and Some Spirits.* London, 1659. Reprinted London: Askin, 1974. Reprinted with Introduction by Lon Milo DuQuette. New York: Magickal Childe Publishing Inc., 1992.

Crowley, Aleister. [*Book Four.*] *Magick. Book Four, Parts I–IV.* ed. Hymenaeus Beta. York Beach, ME: Samuel Weiser, 1994.

———. *The Book of Lies.* York Beach, ME: Samuel Weiser, 1992.

———. *The Book of Thoth. A Short Essay on the Tarot of the Egyptians.* The Master Therion. London: O.T.O., 1944. *The Equinox* III(5). Reprinted York Beach, ME, Samuel Weiser, 1992.

———. *The Equinox* I(8). Fall 1912, ed. Soror Virakam, London. Reprinted York Beach, ME: Samuel Weiser, 1992.

———. *The Equinox* III(5). Spring 1944, *The Book of Thoth.* See entry under book title.

———. *The Equinox* III(6). Fall 1961, *Liber Aleph.* See entry under book title.

———. *The Equinox* III(7). 1971, *Shih Yi.* See entry under book title.

———. *The Equinox* III(9). Spring 1983, [*Thelema*] ΘΕΛΗΜΑ: *The Holy Books of Thelema.* See entry under book title.

———. [*Goetia.*] *The Book of the Goetia of Solomon the King*, ed. Aleister Crowley. Foyers, Scotland: Society for the Propagation of Religious Truth, 1904. Reprinted New York: Magickal Childe Publications, 1989.

———. *Konx Om Pax*. Foyers, Scotland: Society for the Propagation of Religious Truth, 1907. Reprinted with an Introduction by Martin P. Starr, Chicago: The Teitan Press, 1990.

———. *Liber Aleph vel CXI. The Book of Wisdom or Folly*, ed. Karl Germer and Marcelo Motta. Barstow, CA: Thelema Publishing Co., 1961. *The Equinox* III(6) Rev. 2d edition, ed. Hymenaeus Beta. York Beach, ME: Samuel Weiser, and New York: 93 Publishing, 1991).

———. *Little Essays Toward Truth*. London: O.T.O. 1936. Reprinted Scottsdale, AZ: New Falcon Publications, 1991.

———. *Magick*. See *Book 4*.

———. *Magick in Theory and Practice (Book 4, Part III)*. Paris: Lecram Press, 1929–30. Most recent facsimile reprint, New York: Magickal Childe Publications, 1990. See also *Book 4*.

———. *Magick without Tears*, ed. Israel Regardie. Scottsdale, AZ: New Falcon Publications, 1991.

———. *777 and Other Qabalistic Writings*, ed. Israel Regardie. York Beach, ME: Weiser, 1993.

———. *Shih Yi*, ed. H. Parsons Smith. Oceanside, CA: Thelema Publications, 1971. *The Equinox* III(7).

——— (received by). [*Thelema*] ΘΕΛΗΜΑ: *The Holy Books of Thelema*, ed. Hymenaeus Alpha and Hymenaeus Beta. York Beach, ME: Weiser, 1983. *The Equinox* III(9). Corrected 2nd printing (York Beach, ME: Samuel Weiser, and New York: 93 Publishing, 1990).

———. *The Collected Works of Aleister Crowley*, ed. I. Back. Foyers, Scotland: Society for the Propagation of Religious Truth, 1905–1907. Reprinted Homewood, IL: Yogi Publication Society, c. 1978.

DuQuette, Lon Milo. *The Magick of Thelema*. York Beach, ME: Samuel Weiser, 1993.

——— and C. S. Hyatt. *Aleister Crowley's Illustrated Goetia*. Scottsdale, AZ: New Falcon Publications, 1992.

——— and C. S. Hyatt. *Enochian World of Aleister Crowley*. Scottsdale, AZ: New Falcon Publications, 1991.

———— and C. S. Hyatt. *The Way of the Secret Lover: Tantra, Tarot and the Holy Guardian Angel.* Scottsdale, AZ: New Falcon Publications, 1991.

James, William. *The Varieties of Religious Experience.* London: Longmans, 1910; New York: Random House, 1993.

Jung, Carl G. *Man and His Symbols.* London: Aldus Books, 1964; New York: Dell, 1968.

Laycock, Donald C. *The Complete Enochian Dictionary. A Dictionary of the Angelic Language as revealed to Dr. John Dee and Edward Kelley.* London: Askin Publishers, 1978. Reprinted York Beach, ME: Samuel Weiser, 1994.

Lévi, Éliphas. *The Key of the Mysteries,* trans. Aleister Crowley. York Beach, ME: Samuel Weiser, 1970; London: Rider & Co., 1969. Also as special supplement to *Equinox* I(10).

————. *The History of Magic,* trans. Arthur Edward Waite. London: Rider, 1957; New York: Samuel Weiser, 1970.

————. *Transcendental Magic: Its Doctrine and Ritual,* tr. Arthur Edward Waite. London: Rider & Co., 1896; York Beach, ME: Samuel Weiser, 1968.

Mathers, S.L. MacGregor. trans. *The Book of the Sacred Magic of Abra-Melin the Mage.* New York: Dover Publications, Inc., 1975.

————, trans. *The Kabbalah Unveiled.* York Beach, ME: Samuel Weiser, 1974.

McLean, Adam. ed. *A Treatise on Angel Magic.* Grand Rapids, MI: Phanes Press, 1990.

Ponce, Charles. *Kabbalah.* San Francisco: Quest Books, 1983.

Regardie, Israel. *The Golden Dawn.* 6th edition. St. Paul: Llewellyn Publications, 1992.

Stirling, William. *The Canon.* London: R.I.L.K.O., 1974.

Suares, Carlo. *The Sepher Yetsira,* trans. Micheline & Vincent Stuart. Boston: Shambhala, 1976.

Turner, Robert. *Elizabethan Magic.* Shaftesbury, England, Element Books, Ltd. 1989.

Wang, Robert. *An Introduction to the Golden Dawn Tarot.* York Beach, ME: Samuel Weiser, 1978.

————. *The Qabalistic Tarot.* York Beach, ME: Samuel Weiser, 1983.

Zalewski, Pat. *Kabbalah of the Golden Dawn.* St. Paul: Llewellyn Publications, 1993.

Although Lon Milo DuQuette takes the subject of ceremonial magick very seriously, he tries to remember not to take himself too seriously. This rare combination of common sense and humor have, in the last ten years, earned him a respectable position in the world of modern occultism.

In 1991 he was asked by noted author and occultist, Christopher S. Hyatt, Ph.D., to co-author a series of books dealing with the fundamental concepts and psychological implications of Enochian Magick, Goetic Evocation, Tarot, and Sex Magick.[1]

In 1992 he was privileged to be invited by Magickal Childe Publishing to write a new introduction to the re-issue of one of the most significant magical texts of all time, Meric Casaubon's 1659 *A True and Faithful Relation of What Passed for Many Years Between Dr. John Dee and Some Spirits....*[2] He has also written and narrated a 60 minute video, *Enochian Magick, The Art of Angelic Evocation.*[3]

With the *Tarot of Ceremonial Magick* DuQuette visually shares his magical understanding and experience through the qabalistic matrix of the Tarot. Drawn by DuQuette and painted by his wife Constance, the cards are a wealth of information directly related to the practical applications of Enochian Magick, Goetic Evocation, and Astrology.

Lon and Constance DuQuette live with their son, Jean-Paul, in Newport Beach, California.

1. *Enochian World of Aleister Crowley* (1991), *Aleister Crowley's Illustrated Goetia* (1992), *Way of the Secret Lover* (1991), and *Taboo* (1992); Scottsdale, AZ: New Falcon Publications.
2. New York: Magickal Childe Publishing, 1992.
3. Claremont, CA: Hooded Man Productions, 1994.

Paul J. Maska